MASKS

TEN AMAZING MASKS
TO ASSEMBLE AND WEAR

CHRISTOS KONDEATIS

ATLANTIC MONTHLY PRESS
New York

This book was designed and produced by
Genesis Productions Limited,
30 Great Portland Street, London W1N 5AD

First published in the USA 1987 by Atlantic Monthly Press, New York

ISBN 0-87113-172-2

Devised by Christos Kondeatis and Jeremy Cox

Design, illustrations and paper engineering: Christos Kondeatis

Assistant designer: Jane Ewart

Text: Elizabeth Cooper

Editor: Esther Jagger

Printed and bound in Colombia

TUTANKHAMUN

Tutankhamun, whose name means "the living image of Amon", lived in the fourteenth century BC. He was the young Pharaoh or ruler of Egypt at this time. He had married a daughter of the famous Pharaoh Akhenaten and probably came to the throne when he was only a boy about twelve years old.

The Pharaoh Akhenaten had tried to make the Egyptians worship only one god, the sun-god Aton. Tutankhamun, who was originally called Tutankhaten, changed his name to show that he wished to restore the worship of the great god Amon. However, it seems likely that the powerful priests of Amon hated the young king as much as they had hated his father-in-law.

At the time Tutankhamun was probably not a very important Pharaoh, but he is famous now because his is the only Egyptian royal tomb to have survived with its contents virtually intact. When he died at about the age of eighteen, his tomb was not built beneath a pyramid because the pyramid tombs were already being plundered by grave robbers. Instead it was cut into the cliffs along the river Nile. Two hundred years later the men who were building the tombs of a later Pharaoh above Tutankhamun's tomb threw their rubbish down into it and buried it completely.

More than three thousand years later, on 4 November 1922, the British archeologist Howard Carter uncovered the steps leading down to the burial chambers of the boy Pharaoh. It was the greatest moment in Carter's life when, three weeks later, he and his team broke through into the chambers of the tomb. They found hundreds of beautiful objects, jewels and pieces of furniture all carved, painted, covered in precious stones and richly gilded. This astonishing treasure, which took many months to excavate, showed for the first time what the court of a Pharaoh of ancient Egypt must have been like.

A year or so later, inside a red sandstone sarcophagus, Carter found a nest of three coffins each carved and decorated to look like the mummified body of the young king. The two outer coffins were made of gilded wood, the innermost one of solid gold. Inside it was the mummy itself, wearing a beautiful death mask made of gold and inlaid with semi-precious stones and blue glass.

Like all the kings of ancient Egypt, Tutankhamun was worshipped as a living god, but he was only human. Painted scenes in the tomb show him sitting at home with his young wife and hunting wildfowl along the Nile. It is not known how or why he died so young, but he may have been murdered by the priests of Amon. After his death they tried to remove all mention of his name from statues and inscriptions.

At the time of the discovery of Tutankhamun's tomb people began saying that a curse had been put upon it. Howard Carter's patron, Lord Carnarvon, and two other members of his team fell ill and died only a few months after the burial chamber had been opened. Lord Carnarvon never saw the mummy and its famous mask. At the very moment of his death all the electric lights in Cairo mysteriously went out, and back in England his pet dog is said to have given a terrible howl and then died too. However, Howard Carter himself lived on until 1939.

Tutankhamun had a short reign, probably only six years, but thanks to Howard Carter the boy Pharaoh is now immortal.

Tutankhamun's gold death mask, thought to be an exact likeness of the boy Pharaoh. A curse was said to have been laid on anyone who entered his magnificent tomb.

CARNIVAL MASK

Carnival is a Christian festival which used to take place in many countries just before the fasting period called Lent. It originated in very early times when ceremonies were held to celebrate spring fertility.

The word "carnival" is said to come from the Latin words "*carne vale*" which mean "farewell to the flesh", because eating meat during Lent was forbidden by the Church. Feasting, games and noisy behaviour were all part of the carnival fun, and people often wore masks and elaborate fancy dress.

There are a number of modern versions of carnival, including the celebrations in Venice and the Mardi Gras in New Orleans, where people wear fancy dress and masks. The custom of eating pancakes on Shrove Tuesday is also related to carnival. As Shrove Tuesday was the day before the beginning of Lent, it was the last occasion on which foods using animal fats could be eaten.

The wearing of masks at carnival time dates back to the more ancient spring festival, when gods, spirits and dead souls were believed to return to earth for a day. The personalities of these beings were thought to be transferred in some magical way to the wearers of the masks. But by the time this festival had developed into carnival the purpose of the masks had changed – they were meant as a disguise. Everyone took part in carnival, and behind such a disguise even the most important person could act the fool without being recognized.

From the fun of carnival developed a kind of theatre which was popular in sixteenth-century Italy. It was known as the *commedia dell'arte* and consisted of witty comedy with music, dancing and acrobatics. The actors had no scripts but made up the words and the plot as they went along.

The action of *commedia dell'arte* always revolved around the same characters. The best-known of these was Harlequin, or Arlecchino in Italian, who has given his name to modern carnival costumes and masks. Harlequin wore a patchwork costume with a black mask to hide his eyes. He was a clever servant and in love with another servant called Columbine who was also dressed in patchwork. There were other characters too. Pulcinello was an expert at disguise and could appear as a peasant, a doctor or yet another servant. Brighella, in green mask and costume to suggest his wily nature, was a cunning, clever manservant and also a thief. Pierrot, in a loose white costume and with a powdered white face, was a servant who never spoke, while Pantalone was a boastful old man constantly falling in love but always rejected.

Many of the same characters can be seen in modern-day theatre, for example in pantomime and Punch and Judy shows. At the circus we can still be entertained by Pierrot, who has turned into a clown with baggy clothes and chalk-white make-up.

A modern version of a harlequin mask which might be worn at carnival time in Venice.

MEDUSA

In ancient Greek mythology, Medusa was the chief of three terrifying sisters called the Gorgons. She was one of the most frightening monsters of all, although she had once been beautiful. To punish Medusa, the goddess Minerva had transformed her hair into a mass of living snakes, and any human being who looked at her was instantly turned to stone.

The other Gorgons were immortal, but Medusa was not and would die one day. However, she seemed to be protected from death by her power of turning men to stone.

One of the Greek heroes was Perseus. When he was a young man, his mother was a captive of the evil king Polydektes. Perseus tried to free her by saying that he would bring Polydektes the head of Medusa in exchange. This was a very rash promise to make even though he had been given winged shoes and a cap which made him invisible. He would need more help than this when he came face to face with the invincible Gorgons, so he decided to put his trust in the great goddess Athena who had promised him her help.

Perseus sailed across the ocean and came at last to the land where the Gorgons lived. In this dark, gloomy place he found the three Gorgons asleep in a cave, but he knew that if he looked directly at them he would be turned to stone.

The goddess Athena now kept her promise and came to his aid. She made him look at Medusa's reflection in his shield so that he could cut off the monster's head without being harmed.

The blood from Medusa's severed head poured on to the ground, and from it sprang the two children whom she had conceived by the sea-god Poseidon. One of these was the warrior hero Chrysaor, of whom little more is heard, and the other was the winged horse Pegasus. Without delay, Perseus threw Medusa's head into a bag and jumped on to the back of the winged horse. He was soon far away and safe from the remaining two Gorgons.

For some reason Perseus chose not to keep his promise to deliver Medusa's head to King Polydektes, and set off instead on a series of adventures. The head still had its deadly power of turning men to stone, and Perseus used it as a weapon against his enemies. He saved the beautiful Princess Andromeda from her fate as a human sacrifice to an evil dragon and, in seeking her hand in marriage, had to fight off rival suitors. They were turned to stone by the head of Medusa.

Later, in thanks, Perseus gave the head to Athena who placed it in the centre of her shield. It can still be seen today on the shield of the great goddess in Greek statues.

So firmly did the ancient Greeks believe in the powerful magic of Medusa's head that they wore images of it as amulets to ward off evil. Medusa lived on in another way too – the name "Medusa Head" was given to a cluster of stars belonging to the constellation of Perseus.

The head of Medusa, surrounded by writhing, living snakes. In Greek legend, one glance at her face would turn a person into stone.

GARGOYLE

Staring down at people from lofty positions on cathedrals and churches all over Europe are many strange, long-necked creatures of stone. Some look like animals or birds, some are like people, some seem to be a combination of both. They are grim and forbidding with large, glaring eyes, heavy brows and gaping or leering mouths, and some are sticking out their tongues.

These statues are called grotesques or gargoyles and belong to the medieval Gothic style of architecture. In the Middle Ages religion played a very important part in the lives of the common people. Among them were stonemasons, sculptors, ironworkers, glassworkers and carpenters who all believed so strongly in the glory of God that they spent years building and decorating magnificent churches in which to worship Him.

One such religious building is Notre-Dame Cathedral in Paris. The building was begun in 1163, during the reign of King Louis VII, and completed nearly two hundred years later. By the nineteenth century it was sadly in need of repair and in 1841 a team of men led by Viollet-le-Duc began to restore it to its former grandeur. They worked on the glass and the roof, added new statues and restored some of the old gargoyles. It took them twenty-three years.

Viollet-le-Duc thought that the first gargoyles were probably carved in Paris in the thirteenth century. They were made then to perform a special function – to carry away from the roof of the cathedral rainwater which would otherwise run down and wear away the stonework. The head of the creature became a waterspout fed by a channel. Stone heads in animal and human form had been used as waterspouts as long ago as Greek, Roman and ancient Egyptian times.

One of the grotesque beasts' heads that decorate the Cathedral of Notre-Dame in Paris.

Later in the Middle Ages gargoyles were made just for decoration and not to carry water. There were different types: some consisted of a single animal's head or body; others were made up of several figures. Among the animal likenesses were monkeys, panthers, lions, bears, pigs, dogs and sheep; among the human forms were knights, nuns, monks and pilgrims.

Some people believe that the stonemasons were influenced in their choice of subjects by classical stories from ancient Greece and Rome; others think that the Bible provided many subjects; some believe that the ideas came from the remains of prehistoric monsters which were dug up in the Middle Ages. Yet others think that the subjects came mostly from events in daily life, such as the Saints' Days and religious processions, the Mystery Plays which were performed inside the church, special ceremonies such as the Feast of Fools at which there was riotous dancing and singing, and the folk tales of the period.

It seems likely that much of medieval grotesque art has its origins in pre-Christian times, in the pagan beliefs of the Celts, the Greeks and the Romans. These old beliefs, with their legends and symbols, were passed on through the ages and absorbed into the faith of the early Christians.

People believed that carved heads on churches or outside houses had the power to protect the building by keeping away anything that was unlucky or evil. The expressions on the faces were deliberately frightening. What evil being would be brave enough to venture near the menacing head of a lion with a human face, or a fierce-looking beast with monkey features?

THE DEVIL

Satan, or the Devil, is regarded as the source of all evil and the enemy of God. He was originally one of the angels in both Christianity and Islam, and was then known as Lucifer, which means "the light-bearer". Lucifer refused to admit that he depended on God for his happiness and was expelled from Heaven for the sin of pride.

In the Old Testament there is an angel called "the satan", which is Hebrew for "adversary". He tried to persuade God that human beings are evil. Some Christian writers believed that it was the Devil, in the guise of a serpent, who tempted Adam and Eve in the Garden of Eden and so brought evil into the world.

The Book of Revelation in the New Testament brings all these legends together and speaks of a war in Heaven. It describes the Devil as a "great serpent" and an "accuser" who was thrown out of Heaven by other angels.

Satanism, or Devil-worshipping, has had followers for many centuries. It is the very opposite of all that Christians believe in. To Satanists the Devil is God. For morality they substitute immorality, for love of one's fellow-men hatred, for belief in an afterlife power in this world, and so on.

Very often, however, the so called Devil-worshippers were nothing of the kind. They were simply Christians whose way of worshipping was disapproved of by another group of Christians. In the Middle Ages many breakaway groups were cruelly persecuted on this account.

Witchcraft has always been seen as one of the ways in which the Devil acquires power over innocent people. The legend of the witch on her broomstick is known to everyone. There are two days in the year when witches are supposed to come together for feasting and wild dancing. These are Walpurgis Night (30 April) and Hallowe'en (31 October). These festivals go back over a thousand years to the times when people worshipped pagan deities such as the gods of the sun, the moon, fire and water.

The Devil was supposed to appear at these festivals in the form of a goat, and there are two possible reasons for this. One is that a goat was always considered to be an unclean animal, and so made a very suitable disguise for the Devil. The other is that the Devil became confused in people's minds with Pan, the Greek god of nature, who is always represented with the upper body of a man and the lower body and legs of a goat. After the arrival of Christianity such pagan gods as Pan were seen as enemies of the new religion.

Any woman who was old, lived alone or behaved in an odd way was in danger of being accused of witchcraft. Large sums of money were paid to people called "witch-finders" who sought them out. A woman accused of being a witch was always assumed to be guilty unless she could prove her innocence, and was often tortured horribly to make her confess. If a witch was still alive after being tortured, she was frequently burnt to death or hanged. Country areas such as East Anglia in England, and Massachusetts in America, were the scenes of terrible witch-hunts in the sixteenth and seventeenth centuries.

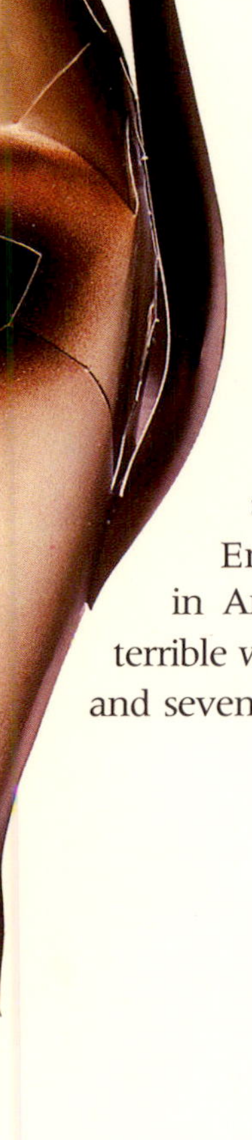

At witches' gatherings on Walpurgis Night or Hallowe'en, the Devil was supposed to appear in the shape of a goat.

CHINESE DRAGON MASK

The dragon is a legendary beast about which many stories have been told and written for hundreds of years. It appears in the folk tales of many different countries and is always a mixture of various creatures. In ancient Egypt it was something like a crocodile, in India it has the features of an elephant, and in China it has the head of a camel, the horns of a stag and the ears of a cow.

In the mythology of the Sumerians, a people who settled in Mesopotamia (modern Iraq) about five thousand years BC, there is a water monster called Zu. This creature may have been the inspiration for the dragons of all other cultures. The story of Zu being killed by the Sumerian sun-god is thought to have given rise to all sorts of other myths about battles between dragons and sun-gods.

The idea of the dragon travelled westwards to the Mediterranean where it became part of Greek mythology. The Greeks believed that the only way to stop a dragon from destroying all in its path was to sacrifice a young girl of royal blood. Andromeda was such a girl, but was rescued from her fate by the hero Perseus (*see* Medusa, page 4). The Greeks also believed that dragon's teeth that were sown in the ground like seeds would grow into men who would found cities. It was at this time too that dragons were first thought to be the guardians of great hoards of treasure.

Like lions, bulls, elephants and other powerful beasts, dragons were thought to pass on their strength to those who were in contact with them. Drinking a dragon's blood or eating its heart were said to protect a person from harm. In Teutonic myth the hero Siegfried gained such strength by bathing in the blood of a dragon.

In the East the dragon is less forbidding and is not usually connected with evil. The Chinese believe that, like the unicorn, phoenix and tortoise, the dragon is a creature which brings good fortune, although it was once thought that it could cause a drought or an eclipse of the sun if it were offended.

Many centuries ago the dragon became an imperial symbol of the Chinese. During the Manchu dynasty, which lasted from 1644 to 1912, it was used to decorate almost everything to do with the Emperors, including the flag and the throne.

The dragon is still an important feature of Chinese life. The people hold special dragon festivals and include enormous mock dragons in their processions at Chinese New Year. Inside these dragons are people who wear a dragon "body" and mask. These colourful festivals can be seen in cities where there is a large Chinese community, such as London and San Francisco.

A Chinese dragon mask of the kind worn during the Chinese New Year celebrations. It has a camel's head, a stag's horns and a cow's ears.

AFRICAN MASK

The masks worn by many African tribes, especially those in West Africa, are colourful and exotic. They are not usually meant to disguise the wearer, unlike the masks of native tribes in other parts of the world. Nor are they expected to pass on to him the special qualities of the animal or bird which they may represent. Their main function is to indicate a person's social standing.

A mask is often worn, for instance, by the new chief of a tribe when he is installed. Adolescent boys and girls wear them at ceremonies to admit them to adulthood. In some tribes horned masks are worn by young men who organize large hunting parties and are eager to prove their manhood and bravery. Elsewhere, horns on a mask or head-dress may contain magical substances showing that the wearer is the healer or witchdoctor of his tribe or village.

Masks are not always worn for such serious purposes. Some are worn in fun as part of dressing up. Sometimes, when the face and body are elaborately made up, masks are not needed at all.

The carving of a wooden mask or other sculpture must be done with great care, for spirits are believed to live in the trees from which the pieces are carved and must always be treated with respect. If the carver fails to show this respect he may be struck down by misfortune.

There are very strict rules about who may and may not look at masks in African tribes. Some carvings are kept hidden from all the people of the tribe, some just from the women. In some cases no one is meant to see the mask. Then the mask is more like a head-dress, with the important carvings and decorations on top of the head, pointing straight at the sky and the spirits themselves. The front part of the mask is concealed from onlookers by a kind of ruff.

Some masks are made ugly on purpose so that people will not want to see them. Pregnant women are advised not to look at them in case their babies are born with the same ugly features. The Kalabari tribe use ugly masks to drive away evil spirits, and have no beautiful masks at all.

The importance of a mask within a tribe may not always depend upon its appearance or the amount of decoration on it. Sometimes a plain, simple mask is very highly valued because it has proved effective in the past. An old, inherited mask is better than a new one because it has a history of success and the owner feels that he is favoured by his ancestors. Masks that do not seem to work are often thrown away.

African masks and other sculptures are now highly valued as works of art by European collectors. At the beginning of our century they influenced such modern artists as Picasso. But those who value them as works of art may never see them as they were meant to be seen – as part of a ceremony with music, changing in appearance as the wearers move and dance in the shadows cast by fires and torches. Then the carver of one of these masks can look upon it and know that it is a good one and that it is inhabited by spirits.

A horned, wooden mask of the Central African Northern Ba Kete tribe. It is worn by boys at their celebrations on entering manhood.

THE MINOTAUR

The Minotaur was a creature in Greek mythology. It was a strange-looking beast with the head of a bull and the body of a man. Its mother was Pasiphae, wife of Minos, King of the island of Crete. Its father was the Cretan Bull, a superb white bull sent by the sea-god Poseidon to Minos for sacrifice. A special home was built for the Minotaur by the great inventor and craftsman Daedalus. It was a vast maze, called the Labyrinth, in which the creature lay hidden, killing and devouring young men and women for its food. These young people were sent to King Minos as tribute, for in those days Crete was much stronger than Athens.

One of the young men sent from Athens to Crete as an offering to the Minotaur was called Theseus. The daughter of King Minos, Ariadne, fell in love with Theseus and gave him a sword with which to kill the Minotaur and a long thread to leave as a trail as he went further and further into the depths of the Labyrinth.

Theseus was successful. He killed the Minotaur and, following his trail, managed to find his way safely out of the terrible maze.

The story of the Minotaur probably derives from ancient religious cults involving bulls. King Minos himself had been fathered by Zeus in the form of a bull, and he defended his kingdom against his enemies with the help of Talos, a giant with a bull's head. Bullfights were held in Crete, as well as a strange activity called horn grappling, in which young athletes, both men and woman, performed dangerous gymnastic feats with a charging bull.

A silver bull mask, with gold inlay and a scene in relief of the death of the Minotaur. A similar mask would have been worn by people taking part in a Cretan bull ceremony.

Man and bull have been rivals since earliest times. In his hunt for food, primitive man first had to kill the fierce bull which was master and defender of the wild herd. A relationship of mutual fear and awe developed between man and bull. Both were strong and powerful and each was capable of killing the other. The bull's role was to increase the herd and so, to primitive man, it became a symbol of fertility as well as strength.

All early civilizations, such as those in Egypt, India and Mesopotamia, treated the bull with immense respect and frequently made it one of their gods. Gradually these ideas moved westwards to the Mediterranean region. In Crete the bull god was associated with earthquakes. In Greece bulls played an important part in colourful festivals which later developed into Greek theatre. In the Roman world followers of the religion of Mithraism, which preceded Christianity, believed they could purge themselves of their sins by washing in the blood of a dying bull. Something of these ancient bull ceremonies can be seen today in the bullfights of southern Europe and Latin America.

AMERICAN INDIAN SPIRIT MASK

As long as people have been on the earth they have made clothing and ornaments from the hair, fur, skin, teeth, feathers and claws of animals and birds. Primitive tribes believe that the creature's special qualities, such as bravery, speed or long life, will be passed on to the human wearer. The Masai of East Africa, for instance, wear lions' manes, while certain North American Indian tribes have been known to wear head-dresses and costumes made from eagles' feathers.

Eagles were particularly important to the Indians. In some tribes, the braves would add an eagle's feather to their head-dress for each man they killed. An annual Eagle Dance was held by the Pueblo Indians of the south-west. They kept a number of eagles for a year and then sacrificed them so that they could carry messages from earth to the gods.

The American Indians always lived in close communion with nature. In their mythology all living things had equal importance and were like each other in everything except physical appearances. One clan might claim to be descended from the bear, another from the wolf. Members of the clan would believe that they were bears or wolves in human form, and their dwellings and other possessions would be decorated with pictures of that beast.

The Indians of the north-west coast believed that animals had souls just like men. Some of their ceremonial masks and totem poles were half-animal and half-human. The Indians wore their masks during the festivities of the winter months. As there was no hunting for the tribe, they occupied themselves with dancing, theatrical entertainments and feasting.

The biggest ceremony for the Indians of the north-west coast was the potlatch, which could take many months to prepare. It was always held to celebrate a great event such as a coming of age, the raising of a totem pole or the building of a new house. At the potlatch many gifts were given and received according to people's position within the tribe.

One of the most important figures in an Indian community was the shaman or medicine man. He was both doctor and priest, and it was his task to contact the manitous, or spirits. He wore special clothing made of animal skins and he carried carved charms, a rattle and a drum. He chanted and beat the drum until he fell into a trance. Then he would attempt to capture, in a box known as a soul-catcher, the supernatural beings which caused the illness. The Indians believe that everything in nature, even the soil and the rocks, has supernatural powers. Every aspect of their life – hunting, the weather, the harvest, the increase of the tribe and protection from the spirits of the dead – is subject to the whim of the gods.

An American Indian hawk spirit mask. It has the typical down-turned beak which touches the upper lip, and would be worn by Indians who believed that their ancestors were hawks.

KABUKI CHARACTER

Traditional Japanese theatre has two colourful forms which date back many centuries. They are called Noh and Kabuki. They are both very different from modern Western theatre, making use of exaggerated speech, highly individual facial make-up, flamboyant masks and costumes and much gesturing and posturing.

Noh is the more refined of the two forms of theatre and was derived from religious ceremonies. Kabuki is the theatre of the people, and has always reflected popular tastes.

Before Kabuki began, Japan had been dominated by religion and powerful warlords. Ordinary people were not thought to be important. Now for the first time plays dealt with everyday emotions such as love, hate, anger and jealousy and showed how much ordinary human beings could achieve through their own efforts. All the female roles in these plays are acted by men, similar to the way they were played by boys in the theatre of Shakespeare's time. The characters in the plays are human but are able to perform superhuman feats through divine power.

Kabuki actors wear grotesque, thick white make-up on which bold lines are drawn in different colours. These lines stand for qualities such as strength, goodness and evil. The audience can immediately recognize the nature of the characters by the variations in the make-up. Red indicates a villain, but not a particularly clever one. Blue and black lines on a bluish-white face identify a more evil villain of higher social standing. The lines are always applied over the main facial muscles, to accentuate the actor's own expressions. The hero wears a wig and three oversized swords to make him look fiercer than he really is.

Among the traditional gestures and mimes used in Kabuki is the *nirami*, which is performed by an actor when he is making an important announcement. Most obvious is his cross-eyed glare, but he also makes certain movements with his body. He flings his arms sideways, with the palms outwards and the fingers bent, and with his right leg bent under his body he throws out his left leg and stamps his foot on the ground.

The Kabuki actors wear elaborate wigs and beautifully designed costumes in rich, bright fabrics. The costumes are based on historical ones, but are usually made much larger than life and are very difficult to wear. Like the face make-up, they tell the audience much about the personality and social standing of the characters.

Music is another important part of Kabuki. Several instruments are played, the most common of which is a three-stringed, plucked instrument called a *samisen*. Various drums are also used. The sound of each instrument has a special meaning. When the drum known as the *taiko* is sounded, for example, it signifies weather or the landscape.

Kabuki is a traditional form of theatre which has not changed at all in three hundred years. It is as popular now as it has ever been.

This is the character Sukeroku, the handsome hero of one of the best-known Kabuki dramas. He is wearing the typical bold Kabuki make-up. In the play Sukeroku is in love with a lady called Agemaki. He has to kill his rival, the rich and cunning Ikyu, before he can be united with the one he loves.

AMENDMENTS TO INSTRUCTIONS

MEDUSA (page 28): When attaching pieces 8 and 9 to the face, start by glueing flap 61 in position and work your way backwards. Note that flap 49 glues to areas 48 and 49, flaps 47 and 48 glue to area 47, flap 42 glues to areas 41 and 42, and flaps 40 and 41 glue to area 40.

MINOTAUR (page 46): On piece 5, flap 53 should read 51.

AMERICAN INDIAN (page 48): When glueing piece 2 onto main face, note that flap 42 moves up one place and glues to area 41 (ignore area 42); all other flaps will fall into place. Similarly on piece 3, flap 59 glues to area 58 (ignore area 59).

INSTRUCTIONS

GENERAL INSTRUCTIONS

You will need:

- a strong, all-purpose clear adhesive
- a pin or toothpick are useful, to help you apply glue to small areas with greater accuracy and to avoid glue running on to printed areas
- nail scissors may be useful but are not essential
- elasticated thread to enable you to wear the mask

1. The pieces to make up the masks are die-cut, and all you have to do is press them out from the page. When you have done this you may need to tidy up the edges of the paper with nail scissors.

2. All the mask pieces are numbered on the back [1] , [2] and so on (note that these piece numbers will be represented by a bold figure in the individual instructions). You will find it helpful to press out all the pieces and arrange them in numerical order, because this is the order in which you will use them. **Some of the masks have pieces on two or three separate pages. Always make sure you have pressed out all the pieces.**

3. It is nearly always the white flaps (numbered 1 , 2 , 3 and so on) on the front of the mask to which you should apply the glue. (Exceptions are clearly indicated in the individual instructions.) **Always cover the whole flap with glue.**

Each flap to be glued has a corresponding numbered area marked on the back of the mask. All you need to do is put a little glue on the flap marked 1 on the front of the mask, and then stick it to the area marked 1 on the back of the mask. Then you glue 2 to 2 , 3 to 3 , and so on. **The flaps should always be glued in the order given in the instructions.**

When you start making a mask only glue and stick one flap at a time, because you will need to **hold it in position for at least 30 seconds** to allow the glue to dry properly. This is particularly important with very small flaps, e.g. those underneath the nose.

4. Crease lines are always indicated on the back of the mask by dotted lines and are numbered 1 , 2 , 3 and so on. **Always fold along a crease line with the mask facing you.**

5. Slots are numbered [1] , [2] , [3] and so on.

6. All black-striped areas, e.g. eye sockets, should be pressed out and thrown away.

7. To fasten a mask, find the hole on either side at ear level, and press them both out. (Note that Medusa, the Chinese Dragon and Tutankhamun have **two** holes on each side.) Cut a short length of elasticated thread, press one end through one hole and tie the end in a double knot. Take the thread along the back of the mask, pass it through the other hole and tie another double knot. Now you can wear your mask.

TUTANKHAMUN *See picture on page 3*

Press pieces **1, 2, 5** and **6** out of page 17 and pieces **3, 4, 7, 8, 9, 10, 11** and **12** out of page 20. Press out and throw away the striped areas from the eyes and ears.

Take piece **1,** the face. Start by shaping the eyebrows. With the mask facing you, gently press down and away from you along creases 1 and 2 . Then glue flap 1 and continue with flaps 2, 3 and 4.

Next take piece **2,** the nose. With the front facing you shape it by folding down along creases 3 , 4 and 5 . Then fold flaps 5 and 6 up towards you.

Now attach the nose to the face by glueing flaps 5 and 6 to the inside of the face and inserting flap 7 from the front through slot [1] .

With the front of the mask facing you, press down along creases 6 and 7 to shape the forehead. Then press gently down along creases 8 and 9 for the lips. To shape the head, glue flaps 8 to 20.

To attach the two halves of the upper lip, glue flaps 21 and 22. Do the same on the chin by glueing flaps 23 and 24.

To complete the face apply glue to nose flaps 25, 26 and 27, then to cheek flaps 28 and 29. First stick down flap 25, then position 26, 27, 28 and 29 behind it and stick them down.

Take pieces **3** and **4,** which make up the head-dress. Fold all the flaps firmly up and towards you, then glue flap 30 on piece **3** and flap 31 on piece **4.** Pieces **3** and **4** should form a slightly hollow shape when you have glued these flaps.

Now attach piece **3** to the face by glueing flaps 32 and 33 to the inside of the face **(line up stripes when positioning).** Do the same with flaps 34 and 35 for piece **4** on the other side.

Next take pieces **5** and **6,** the ears. To shape them, start by glueing flaps 36 and 37. Now insert flaps 38 and 39 through slots [2] and [3] respectively on the main mask, and glue them on the inside to hold them in position.

To make the ceremonial beard, take piece **7** and roll it gently so that you can glue flap 40. Then take piece **8,** insert flap 41 through slot [4] , and glue it. Bend piece **8** gently and glue flap 42 inside the back of the beard.

To attach the beard to the chin insert flaps 43 and 44 through slots [5] and [6] respectively. Fold the flaps back and glue them in position.

Finally make the two serpents and attach them to the head-dress Take piece **9,** the first body. Insert flap 45 through slot [7] on the forehead and then back through slot [8] . Glue flap 45. Next take piece **10,** the first head, and fold down along the score marks. Glue flaps 46 together. Now apply glue to area 47 inside the serpent's head, and stick it to the top of piece **9.**

Repeat for the second serpent, using piece **11,** threading flap 48 through slots [9] and [10] , and then glueing flap 48 in position. Take piece **12,** glue flaps 49 together, and then flap 50. Then glue flap 51 to the top of piece **11.**

Fasten elasticated thread through the two holes on one side of the mask and then through the two holes on the other side, knotting the thread firmly.

CARNIVAL MASK *See picture on page 4*

Press pieces **1** to **4** out of page 21. Press out and throw away the striped eye and lip areas.

Take piece **1**, the forehead. With the front of the mask facing you, gently press down and away from you along creases 1 and 2 . This will shape the forehead. Now glue flap 1. When it is firmly stuck, glue flap 2. Then glue, one at a time, flaps 3 to 6.

Take piece **2**, the lower face. With the mask facing you, gently shape the lips by pressing down along crease 3 . Glue flaps 7 and 8, then flaps 9 and 10. Join the lower lip by folding down flaps 11 and 12 and then glueing them in position.

Before joining the two halves of the face you need to prepare the chin and nose. Start by taking piece **3**, the chin. With the mask facing you fold down along creases 4 and 5 . Glue flaps 13 to 17.

Now you are ready to attach the chin to piece **2**. First gently fold flaps 18 to 23 up towards you, then glue them in position behind the lower lip on piece **2**. Now, with the back of the mask facing you, **apply glue to the entire area 24** and stick it to flap 24. Repeat for the other side, **glueing area 25** and sticking it to flap 25.

Now shape the nose. Take piece **4** and, with the mask facing you, fold down and away from you along creases 6 , 7 and 8 . Now gently fold up along creases 9 and 10 .

The nose is now ready to be attached. Glue flap 26 in position behind the forehead. Then glue flaps 27 and 28 to the back of the nose (make sure that flaps 29 and 30 are in front of flaps 31 and 35 when the mask is facing you).

Now you can join the two halves of the mask together. Start by **applying glue to all the areas numbered 29 to 38** at the same time. Then stick them to the corresponding flaps on the sides of the nose. Now glue flap 39 and then flap 40.

With the back of the mask facing you, finish the nose by glueing flaps 41, 42 and 43.

Finally, fold back flaps 44, 45 and 46 and glue them inside the mask. Do the same on the other side with flaps 47, 48 and 49.

Fasten elasticated thread round the back of the mask as described in the general instructions.

MEDUSA *See picture on page 5*

Press pieces **1** and **2** out of page 24, pieces **4, 5, 6** and **7** out of page 25, and Medusa pieces **3, 8** and **9** out of page 28. Press out and throw away all striped areas.

Take piece **1**, the forehead. Shape the eyes by glueing flaps 1 and 2 and then flaps 3 and 4. Continue to shape the forehead by glueing flaps 5 to 9.

Next make up the chin. Take piece **2**, and with the front facing you press gently down along crease 1 to start shaping the lips. Glue flap 10 on the lower lip. Then glue flaps 11 and 12. Form the chin by glueing flaps 13 to 16.

Now you can join the two halves of the face together. Apply glue to flap 17 on piece **2** and stick it in position on the side of the face inside piece **1** **(note that the end of flap 17 slots in between flap 18 and the side of the face).** Next glue flap 18. Now do the same on the other side, glueing flaps 19 and 20.

Take piece **3**, the nose. With the front facing you press down along creases 2 , 3 and 4 and then fold flaps 21 to 28 up towards you.

To attach the nose to the face first apply glue to flaps 24, 25 and 26 and stick them in position.Then apply glue to flaps 21, 22, 23, 27 and 28 and stick them in position.

Now you can start to add the snake pieces to the face. Start with piece **4**, and with the front facing you fold flaps 29 and 30 down. Then fold down flap 31 **(note that it folds down in two places).** Insert flap 29 through slot [1] in the face, fold it back and glue it. Then insert flap 30 through slot [2] , and flap 31 through slot [3] , and stick them in position.

Take piece **5** and insert flap 32 through slot [4] . Then insert flap 33 through slot [5] . Fold both flaps back and glue them in position. Continue with piece **6** by inserting flaps 34 and 35 through slots [6] and [7] respectively, folding them down and glueing them in position. Then go on to piece **7**, inserting flaps 36, 37 and 38 through slots [8] , [9] and [10] respectively, folding them back and glueing them in position.

Finally take pieces **8** and **9** and join them together by glueing flap 39. Fold all flaps 40 to 61 up towards you, so that they are at right angles to the piece. Then glue flaps 40 to 61 to the inside of the face.

To finish the snakes, find flaps 62, 63, 64 and 65 on piece **6** and glue them to the corresponding flaps on piece **8**. Next find flap 66 on piece **7** and glue it to area 66 on the forehead. Do the same with flap 67 on piece **4**, glueing it down to the head. Then find flap 68 on piece **5** and glue it down to the head. Lastly find flaps 69, 70 and 71 on piece **5** and glue them to the corresponding flaps on piece **9**.

Fasten elasticated thread through the two holes on one side of the mask and then through the two holes on the other side, knotting the thread firmly.

GARGOYLE *See picture on page 6*

Press pieces **1, 2, 8, 9** and **10** out of page 29, Gargoyle pieces **3** and **4** out of page 28 and Gargoyle pieces **5, 6** and **7** out of page 32. Press out and throw away all striped areas.

Take piece **1**, and start by shaping the head. With the front of the mask facing you, press gently down along crease 1 . Then press down along creases 2 to 5 . Still with the front facing you, fold up along creases 6 and 7 . Then fold down along creases 8 to 12 .

To shape the forehead glue flaps 1 to 7. Then glue flaps 8 and 9, followed by 10 and 11.

Next fold flaps 12 and 13 up towards you. Then apply glue to flaps 12 to 15 and stick them all in position together. Now glue flaps 16 and 17.

To complete the other side, first fold flaps 18 and 19 up towards you. Apply glue to flaps 18 to 21 and stick them in position. Finish by glueing flaps 22 and 23.

Take pieces **2** and **3**, the chin, and join them together by glueing flaps 24 and 25. Fold flap 26 down and glue it in position.

Now you can join the chin to the face. Glue flaps 27 and 28 on one side, then flaps 29 and 30 on the other.

To make the horn, take piece **4** and glue flap 31 in position on piece **5**. Fold down flaps 32 to 37 and stick them in position. Now attach the horn to the forehead by inserting flaps 38, 39 and 40 through slots [1] , [2] and [3] respectively. Fold the flaps back and glue them in position.

To make the beard, take pieces **6** and **7**. Glue flap 41 in position. Fold flaps 42 to 45 down and glue them in position. Then insert flaps 46, 47 and 48 through slots [4] , [5] and [6] respectively on the chin. Fold the flaps back and glue them in position.

Take piece **8**, the tongue, and glue flap 49. Then take the main mask and, with the back facing you, attach piece **8** by glueing flaps 50 to 54 in position inside the mouth.

Finally attach the ears. Take piece **9**, insert flap 55 through slot [7] and glue it in position. Do the same with piece **10**: insert flap 56 through slot [8] and glue it in position.

Fasten elasticated thread round the back of the mask as described in the general instructions.

THE DEVIL *See picture on page 7*

Press pieces **1** and **2** out of page 33, and Devil pieces **3** to **10** out of page 32. Press out and throw away all the striped areas from the lips, eyes, beard and the sides of the face.

Take piece **1**, the forehead. With the front facing you, start to shape the forehead by pressing down along creases 1 to 7 . Now press up towards you along creases 8 and 9 . Glue flaps 1, 2 and 3, then flaps 4, 5 and 6.

Take piece **2**, the lower face. With the front of the mask facing you start by shaping the bottom part of the eyes. Press down along creases 10 and 11 , then press up towards you along creases 12 and 13 . Now shape the lips by gently pressing down along creases 14 and 15 . Glue flaps 7 to 10, **taking extra care to hold them until they are firmly stuck.**

Shape the chin by glueing flap 11 (make sure the beard is in front of the chin).

Next, join the forehead and lower face together. Start by glueing flaps 12 and 13 in position to secure the inside of the eye. Now do the same to the other eye by glueing flaps 14 and 15.

Join the sides of the face by glueing flaps 16 and 17 on one side, and flaps 18 and 19 on the other side.

Now finish shaping the chin by folding flap 20 inside the face and glueing it in position. Do the same for the other side and glue flap 21.

Complete this stage by folding flaps 22 and 23, which are at the side of the cheeks, right round inside the mask. Then glue them in position.

Now you are ready to make the nose, ears, horns and hair. Take piece **3**, the nose. With the front facing you, start to shape it by pressing down along crease 16 and then down along creases 17 and 18 . Then fold flaps 24 to 33 up towards you.

The nose can now be attached to the face. Apply glue to all flaps 24 to 33 together and start by sticking flaps 30, 31 and 32 in position inside the face. Continue by positioning flaps 24 to 29 and 33. **Note that flaps 29 and 33 stick down on top of flaps 30 and 32.**

Take piece **4**, an ear, and apply glue to flap 34. With the front facing you stick it in position so that the point of the ear slopes gently away from you.

Now take piece **5**, the hair. Insert flap 35 on the ear through slot [1] . Fold back flap 35 and glue it in position.

Now join the ear and hair to the side of the face. Insert flap 36 through slot [2] in the side of the face and glue it in position. Then fold flap 37 over along crease 19 and glue it in position inside the face.

Now repeat for the other side by taking piece **6**, the second ear, and glueing flap 38. Insert flap 39 through slot [3] on piece **7**, fold it back and glue it in position. Now insert flap 40 through slot [4] on the side of the face, and glue it in position. Fold flap 41 over along crease 20 and glue it in position inside the face.

Take piece **8**, the fringe, and with the front facing you fold down along crease 21 . Apply glue to flaps 42 and 43 and stick them inside the forehead so that the fringe hangs down over the face.

Now, with the inside of the mask facing you, glue flap 44 and stick it in position.

You are now ready to make the horns. Take piece **9** and gently roll the top (the end without the three flaps) round to form a cone. Keep rolling the paper until it starts to hold this shape by itself and the whole of flap area 45 is covered by the coloured area. Now glue flap 45 and stick it firmly in place. **You may need to apply glue to both surfaces** to make sure of a good strong join. Hold it firmly until it is securely stuck.

Take this horn and insert flaps 46, 47 and 48 through slots [5] , [6] and [7] respectively on the forehead. Fold them over and glue them to the corresponding numbered areas.

Now do the same with piece **10**. Shape the horn, then glue flap 49 and stick it in position. Insert flaps 50, 51 and 52 through slots [8] , [9] and [10] respectively on the forehead, then fold them over and glue them to the corresponding numbered areas.

Finish by glueing flap 53 to hold the fringe down on the forehead.

Fasten elasticated thread round the back of the mask as described in the general instructions.

CHINESE DRAGON MASK
See picture on page 8

Press pieces **1, 3, 4, 5** and **9** out of page 36, pieces **6, 7, 8, 10, 11, 13** and **14** out of page 37, and Dragon pieces **2** and **12** out of page 40. Press out and throw away all the striped areas.

Take piece **1**, the main face, and with the mask facing you fold up towards you along creases **1** and **2**.

To shape the forehead, glue and stick flap 1, then flap 2 and lastly flaps 3 and 4. When they are firmly stuck glue flap 5, then flap 6.

Take piece **2**, the lower face. Glue and stick flaps 7 and 8. Shape the chin by glueing and sticking flaps 9 and 10.

Now join the two halves of the face together. Apply glue to flap 11 on piece **1** and stick it to flap 11 on the inside of piece **2.** Now glue flap 12, followed by flaps 13 and 14. Continue on the other side by glueing flaps 15, 16 and 17.

Take piece **3**, and with the front facing you fold flaps 18 and 19 up, then insert them through the mouth of the dragon and glue them in position.

Take piece **4**, fold flap 20 up, insert it through slot [1] on the main face and glue it in position. Piece **4** should stick out at right angles to the face.

Now do the same with piece **5**, folding flap 21, inserting it through slot [2] and glueing it in position.

With the front of piece **6** facing you, fold down along crease **3** and then up along crease **4**. Next take piece **7** and, with the front facing you, fold down along crease **5** and up along crease **6**.

Now join the two pieces together by glueing flap 22. To attach it to the forehead, insert flap 23 through slot [3] and flaps 24 and 25 through slots [4] and [5] respectively, and glue them in position.

To make the horns, take piece **8** and, with the back facing you, glue flaps 26 together. Now glue flaps 27 together **(it is a good idea to apply glue to both flaps 27 and then hold the piece very tightly to make sure it is firmly stuck).** Now insert flap 28 through slot [6] on the forehead. Fold the flap back and glue it in position.

Do the same to make the other horn. Take piece **9** and glue flaps 29 together. Then glue flaps 30 together. Insert flap 31 through slot [7], fold back and glue.

To make the ears, take piece **10**. With the front facing you, glue flap 32 in position so that the point of the ear is sloping down and away from you.

Now you can join this ear to the head. First fold down along crease **7** so that it is at right angles to the ear. Apply glue to flap 33 on the ear and stick it to flap 33 on the horn. When flap 33 is firmly stuck insert flap 34 through slot [8], then fold it back and glue it in position.

Next take piece **11**, the other ear, and glue flap 35. Fold down along crease **8**, then attach the ear to the horn by glueing flap 36 in position. Insert flap 37 through slot [9], fold it back and glue it.

Take piece **12**, and with the front facing you fold flap 38 up so that it is at right angles to the rest of the piece. Apply glue to flap 38 and stick it in position at the side of the face. Repeat with piece **13**: fold flap 39 up and glue it in position.

Finally take piece **14** and, with the front facing you, fold up flaps 40 to 55 so that they are at right angles to the piece. Apply glue to all these flaps at once and stick them in position inside the mask.

Fasten elasticated thread through the two holes on one side of the mask and then through the two holes on the other side, knotting the thread firmly.

AFRICAN MASK *See picture on page 9*

Press pieces **1, 2** and **3** out of page 41, and African Mask pieces **4** to **9** out of page 40. Press out and throw away the striped areas from pieces **1** and **6.**

Take piece **1**, the main face. With the front of the mask facing you, shape the eye socket by gently pinching down along creases **1** and **2** so that the sockets are sloping inwards.

Now shape the nose. Again with the front of the mask facing you, fold down along creases **3** and **4**, and then up towards you along creases **5** and **6**. (These folds should be at right angles to each other, so that you end up with a very square-shaped nose.)

Finish the nose by folding down along crease **7** at the bottom of the nose. Glue flaps 1 and 2, which will form the nostrils.

Next glue flaps 3 and 4. With the back of the mask facing you, fold down flap 5 and glue it in position.

Shape the forehead by glueing flaps 6, 7 and 8.

Now join one side of the mask by glueing flap 9. Join the other side by glueing flap 10 in the same way.

With the mask facing you, press back the flaps along crease **8**, which runs all round the bottom and sides of the face. Now glue, one at a time, flaps 11 to 19.

With the back of the mask facing you, glue flap 20, then flap 21. Do the same with flaps 22 and 23 on the other side.

To make and attach the ears, first take piece **2**. With the front facing you, fold flap 24 up towards you and glue it in position. Now insert flap 25 through slot [1] in the main mask and flap 26 through slot [2]. Glue flap 25 down, then fold back flap 26 and glue it down.

Repeat with piece **3**. Fold flap 27 up towards you and glue it in position. Insert flap 28 through slot [3] and flap 29 through slot [4]. Glue flap 28 down, then fold flap 29 back and glue it in position.

To make the eyes, first take piece **4** and glue flap 30. Then, with the front of the eye facing you, gently fold flaps 31 to 46 up towards you. Apply glue to all these flaps at once and glue them in position inside the eye socket.

Repeat with piece **5** for the second eye. Glue flap 47, then gently fold up flaps 48 to 63 and glue them inside the other eye socket.

To make the mouth, take piece **6**. With the front facing you, fold down along crease **9**. Fold in flaps 64 to 67 and glue them in position. Again with the mouth facing you, fold flaps 68 to 71 up towards you. Now from the back of the mask insert the mouth through the hole in the face, and glue flaps 68 to 71 in position.

Next take piece **7**, and with the front facing you fold down and away from you along creases **10** to **14**. Now glue flap 72, then flap 73. When these are firmly stuck glue flaps 74 and 75 in position. Fold back flaps 76 and 77 and glue them in position.

Now you can attach piece **7** to the main face. From the front of the mask insert flap 78 through slot [5] on the forehead. Follow by inserting flaps 79 to 83 through slots [6] to [10] respectively on the forehead. You are now forcing the forehead into a rectangular shape: **to make the task easier fold and press the forehead into the right shape as you go.** When all the flaps are inside, glue them in position.

Lastly make the horns. Take piece **8** and gently form the first horn by rolling the piece into a cone shape, so that you can glue flap 84 in position. Then insert flaps 85 and 86 through slots [11] and [12] respectively at the top of the main mask. Fold them back and glue them in position. Then glue flap 87 in position.

For the second horn take piece **9**. Shape the horn as before and glue flap 88. Insert flaps 89 and 90 through slots [13] and [14] respectively, fold them back and glue them in position. Finally glue down flap 91.

Fasten elasticated thread round the back of the mask as described in the general instructions.

THE MINOTAUR *See picture on page 10*

Press pieces **1, 7** and **9** out of page 44, and pieces **2, 3, 4, 5, 6** and **8** out of page 45. Press out and throw away all striped areas.

Start with piece **1,** the main face. First glue flaps 1 and 2. Then glue flaps 3 and 4 and hold them until they are very firmly stuck.

Next take piece **2,** the nose, which must now be attached to the main face. **Apply glue to area 5** on the nose and stick it to flap 5 on the main face. Now apply glue to flap 6, tuck it behind the front of the nose, and stick it in position. Do the same for flap 7. Then glue flaps 8 and 9 in position behind the nose.

With the back of the mask facing you, gently lift up the five flaps along crease **1** and then the five flaps along crease **2**. Keep the mask in the same position and glue flaps 10 to 14. Then turn the mask to face you and glue flaps 15 to 19. Do the same for the other side, glueing flaps 20 to 29.

Finish shaping the main face by glueing flaps 30 and 31.

Take piece **3,** the mane, and with the front facing you fold down along crease **3**. Then fold up towards you along crease **4**. Fold flaps 32 and 33 down. **(Note that flaps 32 and 33 are also marked 42 and 50.)** Finish shaping this piece by folding downwards along the two scored lines at the end of flap 34.

Now insert flap 34 through slot [1] in the forehead, and glue it in position. Next insert flap 32 through slot [2], and then flap 33 through slot [3]. Glue both these in position. The mane should now be raised up from the forehead.

To make the roll-shaped piece on top of the head, apply glue to flap 35 and stick it to area 35 inside the forehead.

To make the first horn, take piece **4.** Glue flap 36 so that the narrow end of the flap is pointing up rather than down. Then glue flap 37. Make sure that both these flaps are stuck very firmly.

Now shape the horn by rolling and easing it into a cone shape (rolling round a pencil helps) so that you can stick flap 38 in position. **You will find it helpful to glue both flap 38 and area 38 to make a firm bond.** Start sticking at the bottom (the wide end) of the horn and work upwards to the point.

Fold flaps 39, 40 and 41 (at the base of the horn) down and into the centre of the horn. Glue flaps 39 and 40 **(note that flap 41 is never glued).** The horn is now ready to be attached to the head.

Insert flap 42 through slot 2, fold it back and glue it in position. Then apply glue to flap 43 (also marked 55) at the back of the horn, fold it inwards and stick it in position inside the head.

To make the second horn take piece **5.** Glue flaps 44, 45 and 46 in the same way as for the first horn. Fold in flaps 47, 48 and 49 and then glue them **(note that flap 49 is never glued).** Insert flap 50 through slot 3 and glue it. Then glue flap 51 inside the back of the head.

Now take piece **6,** an ear, and glue flap 52 to flap 52 opposite, so that you are folding the flap right over on itself. Fold flap 53 upwards and glue it in position inside the head. Then take piece **7** and fold flaps 54 to 59 up. Glue all these flaps and stick them in position inside the head.

Do the same for the other ear. Take piece **8,** then fold and glue together flaps 60. Fold flap 61 up and glue it inside the head. Take piece **9** and fold up flaps 62 to 67, then glue them inside the head.

Fasten elasticated thread round the back of the mask as described in the general instructions.

AMERICAN INDIAN SPIRIT MASK *See picture on page 11*

Press pieces **1** to **4** out of page 48, and American Indian pieces **5, 6** and **7** out of page 49. Press out and throw away all the striped areas from pieces **1, 4, 5** and **6.**

Take piece **1,** the main face. With the front of the mask facing you, shape the beak by folding flaps 1, 2, 3 and 4 downwards. Repeat with flaps 5 to 20. Then glue flaps 1, 2, 3 and 4 and stick them in position on the back of the mask. Continue by glueing flaps 5 to 8, then 9 to 14, and lastly 15 to 20. Make sure each section is firmly stuck before going on to the next.

To shape the forehead, with the mask facing you pinch gently downwards all the way along crease 1. Repeat with crease 2 on the other side of the forehead. Now glue flap 21 to join the forehead together **(make sure flap 22 is behind flap 21 when the mask is facing you).** Then fold flap 22 upwards and glue it in position. Finish shaping the forehead by glueing flaps 23 and 24.

To shape the cheekbones, with the mask facing you gently pinch downwards along crease 3. Then glue flap 25. Repeat for the other side, shaping crease 4 and glueing flap 26. Again with the mask facing you, press gently downwards along crease 5, and then along creases 6, 7 and 8.

To make the nostrils, take pieces **2** and **3.** Starting with piece **2** facing you, fold crease 9 downwards. Then apply glue to flap 27 and stick it so that flaps 33 and 34 are pointing down and away from you. Glue flaps 28 to 31 in the same way. Now fold flaps 32 to 42 up towards you, **taking care not to fold flap 43 by mistake.** Apply glue to all these flaps at once **(leaving out flap 43, which is never glued),** and stick them to the inside of the cheekbone and beak. **This is easier if done from the back of the mask.**

Now repeat these steps with piece **3.** Fold downwards along crease 10. Glue flaps 44 to 48. Then fold flaps 49 to 59 **(taking care not to fold flap 60 by mistake)** and glue them in position. Complete this stage by securing the position of the nostrils: glue flap 60 to form a bridge inside the beak.

To form the cheeks, start with flap 61 and move it into position, but do not apply glue to it yet. With the mask facing you, gently pinch down along crease 11. As you do this the hollow in the cheek should become clear. You can now glue flap 61. Repeat with the other cheek by pinching down along crease 12 and glueing flap 62.

Finish shaping the cheeks and chin by folding downwards along creases 13 and 14, with the front of the mask facing you as usual. Do the same on the other side with creases 15 and 16.

To make the eyes, start by taking piece **4.** With the front facing you, fold down along creases 17 and 18. Then fold flaps 63 to 79 up towards you. Glue flaps 80 and 81.

The eye is now ready to glue into the socket, but first you must complete the socket by glueing flap 82. When this is secure glue flaps 63 to 79 and stick them in position from the inside of the mask.

Repeat with piece **5,** the other eye. Start by folding down along creases 19 and 20, then fold flaps 83 to 99 upwards, and glue flaps 100 and 101. Glue flap 102 on piece **1** to complete the socket, and then insert the eye, glueing flaps 83 to 99.

To make the lips and chin, take piece **6** and fold downwards along creases 21, 22 and 23. Then fold up and towards you along creases 24 and 25. Now stick, one at a time, flaps 103, 104, 105 and 106, followed by 107, 108, 109 and 110. Next apply glue to flap 111 and glue it in position. Glue flap 112 on the other side.

Now take piece **7** and glue flaps 113 to 116. Fold flaps 117 and 118 up towards you. Then glue flaps 117, 118, 119 and 120 all at once and stick them in position on piece **6.**

Before attaching the lips and chin to the main mask glue flaps 121 to 125, which are on the main mask. Then glue flap 126, which is under the end of the beak.

Now you can attach the lips and chin by inserting flaps 127 and 128 through slots 1 and 2 respectively. Then fold them downwards and glue them in position. Glue flap 129, which is at the base of the chin piece, in position. Continue by inserting flap 130 through slot 3, flap 131 through slot 4, flap 132 through slot 5, and lastly flap 133 through slot 6. From the back of the mask fold all these flaps back and glue them in position.

Finally take flap 134, which is at the end of the beak, fold it behind the upper lip and glue it in position.

Fasten elasticated thread round the back of the mask as described in the general instructions.

KABUKI CHARACTER *See picture on page 12*

Press pieces **1** and **2** out of page 52, and Kabuki pieces **3** to **10** out of page 49. Press out and throw away the striped areas next to the lips.

Take piece **1,** the forehead. With the piece facing you, gently press down along creases 1 and 2. Now glue flaps 1 to 6.

Take piece **2,** the jaw, and glue flaps 7 to 10. With the front facing you, shape the lips by gently pressing down along creases 3 and 4. Glue flap 11, which will hold the lower lip in place. Then glue flaps 12 and 13, which will finish shaping the upper lip.

Now you can join the forehead and jaw, by glueing flaps 14 and 15, then 16 and 17.

Take piece **3,** the nose. With the front facing you, shape the nose by folding downwards along creases 5 and 6, and then down along crease 7. Fold flaps 18 to 33 up towards you.

You can now attach the nose to the face. Start by sticking flap 27 in position, then 18 to 26 followed by 28 to 33.

To make the head-dress, take piece **4** and insert flap 34 into slot 1 on the main mask. Fold back flap 34 and glue it in position. Now insert flaps 35 and 36 through slots 2 and 3, then fold them back and glue them in position. Fold back flaps 37 and 38 and glue them in position inside the mask.

Next take piece **5** and glue flap 39. Then insert flaps 40, 41, 42 and 43 through slots 4, 5, 6 and 7 respectively. Fold each flap down after you insert it, and then glue them all in position.

Do the same with piece **6:** glue flap 44, insert flaps 45, 46, 47 and 48 through slots 8, 9, 10 and 11 respectively, and glue them in position.

Now fold flaps 49 and 50 behind the side of the mask and glue them in position. Do the same for flaps 51 and 52.

To make the headband, start by taking pieces **7** and **8** and join them together by glueing flap 53. Then take piece **9,** and with the front facing you fold up flap 54. Now take piece **10,** and with the front facing you fold up flap 59.

To join the two strips together, first apply glue to flap 55 on piece **9** and stick it to the corresponding area on piece **10.** These two strips should now make a V shape. Lift flap 59 to reveal the two flaps marked 54, and glue them together.

Now start to plait the two strips: apply glue to flap 56 on piece **10,** twist piece **9** over piece **10,** and stick flap 56 to the corresponding area on piece **9.** Continue by applying glue to flap 57 on piece **9,** twisting piece **10** over piece **9,** and sticking flap 57 in position. Do the same with flap 58, twisting piece **9** over piece **10.** You should now have a plaited circle.

Now fold the two flaps marked 60 gently outwards so that you can stick them together. To attach the plaited circle to the headband apply glue to flap 59 and stick in position.

Finally attach the completed headband to the mask by folding flaps 61 and 62 round the sides of the forehead, then glueing them in position.

Fasten elasticated thread round the back of the mask as described in the general instructions.

8
9
11
10
12
13
14
1
2
3
4
28
29
15
21
16
22
7
23
17
19
6
24
5
18
20
36
38
39
37
26
27
25

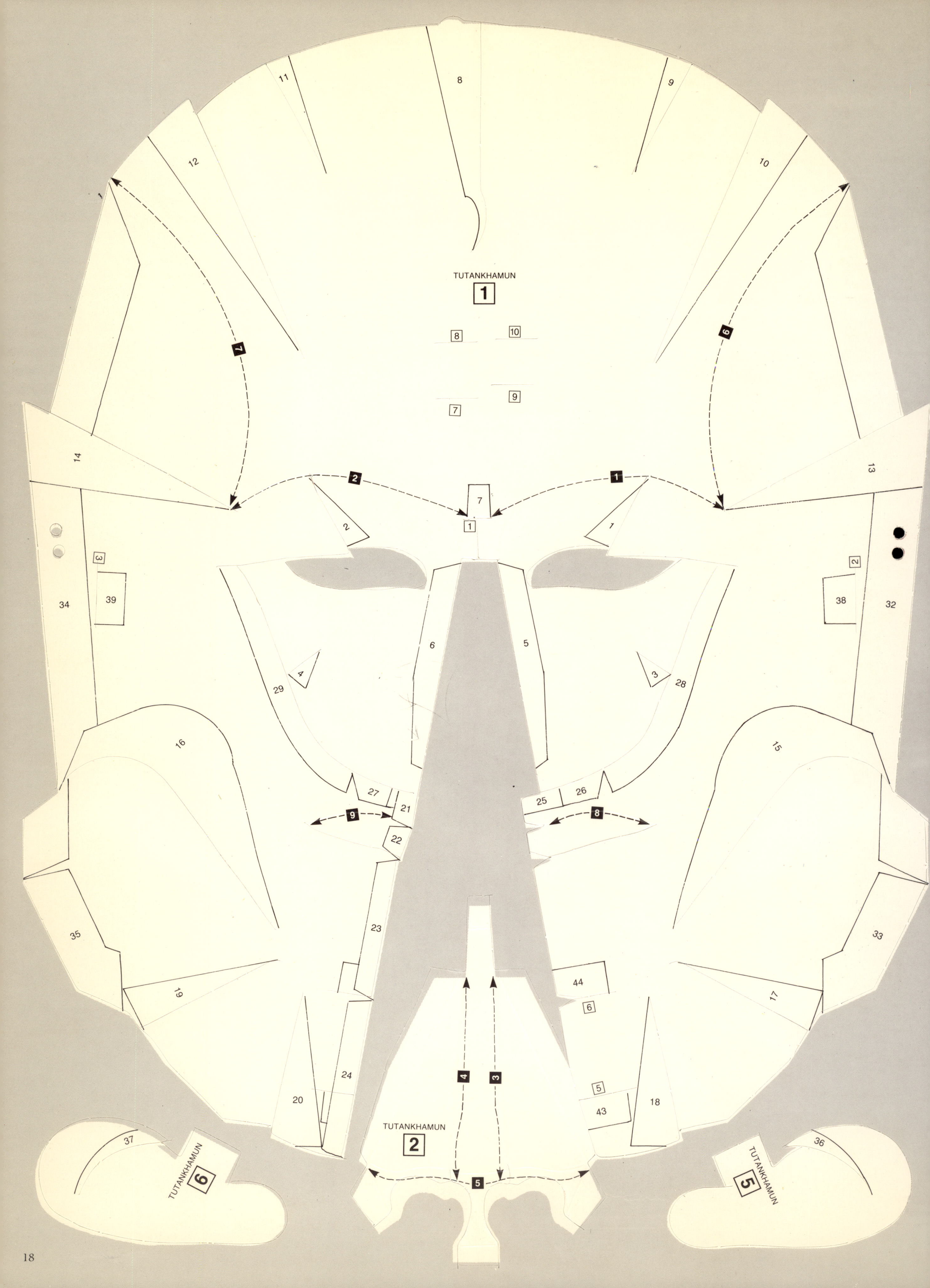
TUTANKHAMUN
1
TUTANKHAMUN
2
TUTANKHAMUN
6
TUTANKHAMUN
5

47
TUTANKHAMUN
10
46
47
50
TUTANKHAMUN
12
49
51
45
TUTANKHAMUN
9
45
51
48
TUTANKHAMUN
11
48
TUTANKHAMUN
4
TUTANKHAMUN
3
30
31
TUTANKHAMUN
8
42
4
41
7
TUTANKHAMUN
40

32
34
50
49
46
33
30
35
31
41
42
40
43
44

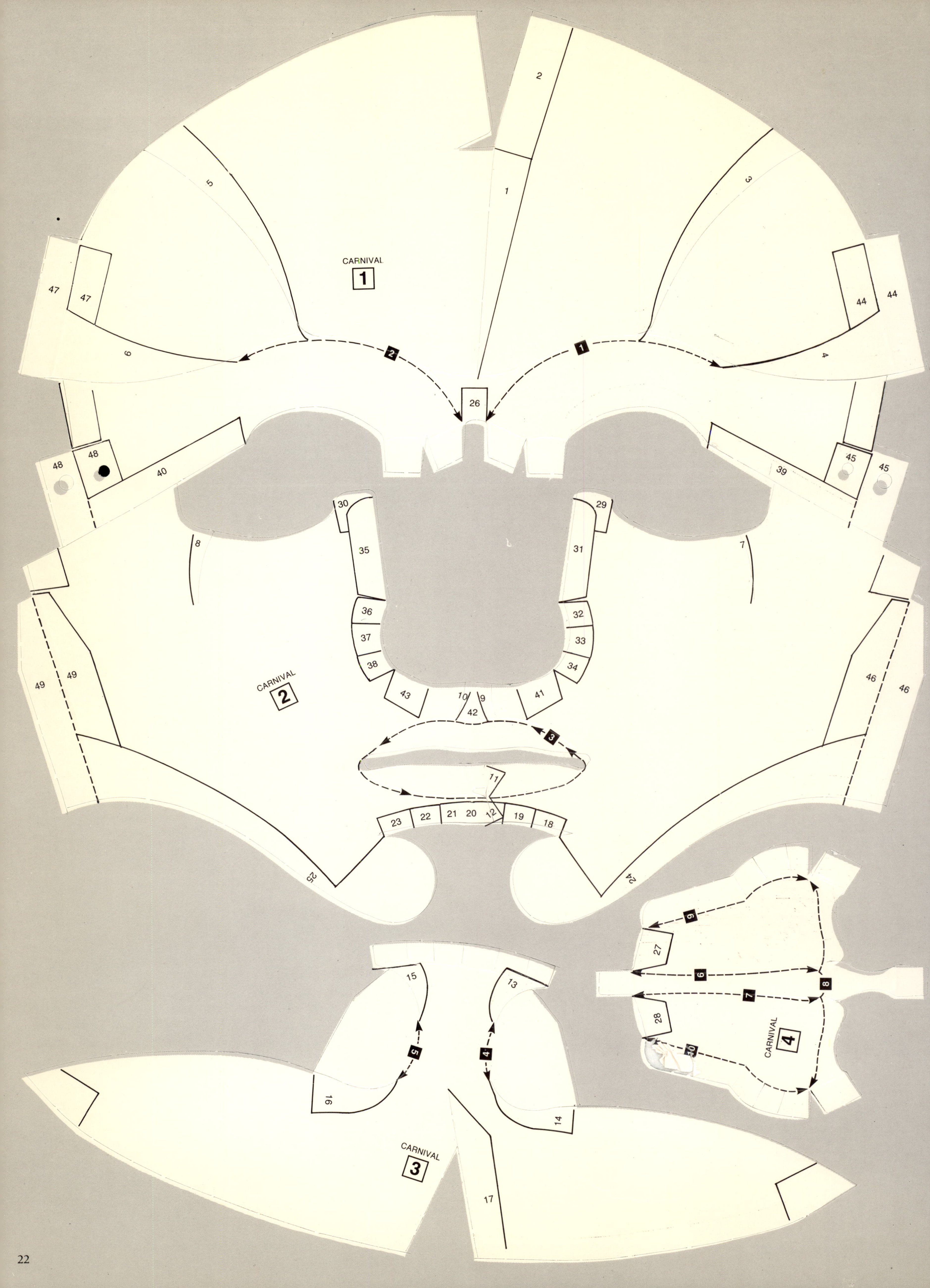

CARNIVAL
1
CARNIVAL
2
CARNIVAL
3
CARNIVAL
4

MEDUSA
1
MEDUSA
2

66
67
68
1
2
3
4
5
6
7
8
9
10
11
12
13
14
15
16
17
18
19
20

MEDUSA 7
MEDUSA 6
MEDUSA 4
MEDUSA 5

63
70
MEDUSA
8
MEDUSA
9
38
GARGOYLE
4
39
39
8
56
51
GARGOYLE
3
2
3
MEDUSA
3
4
5
47
6
48

21
26 25 24

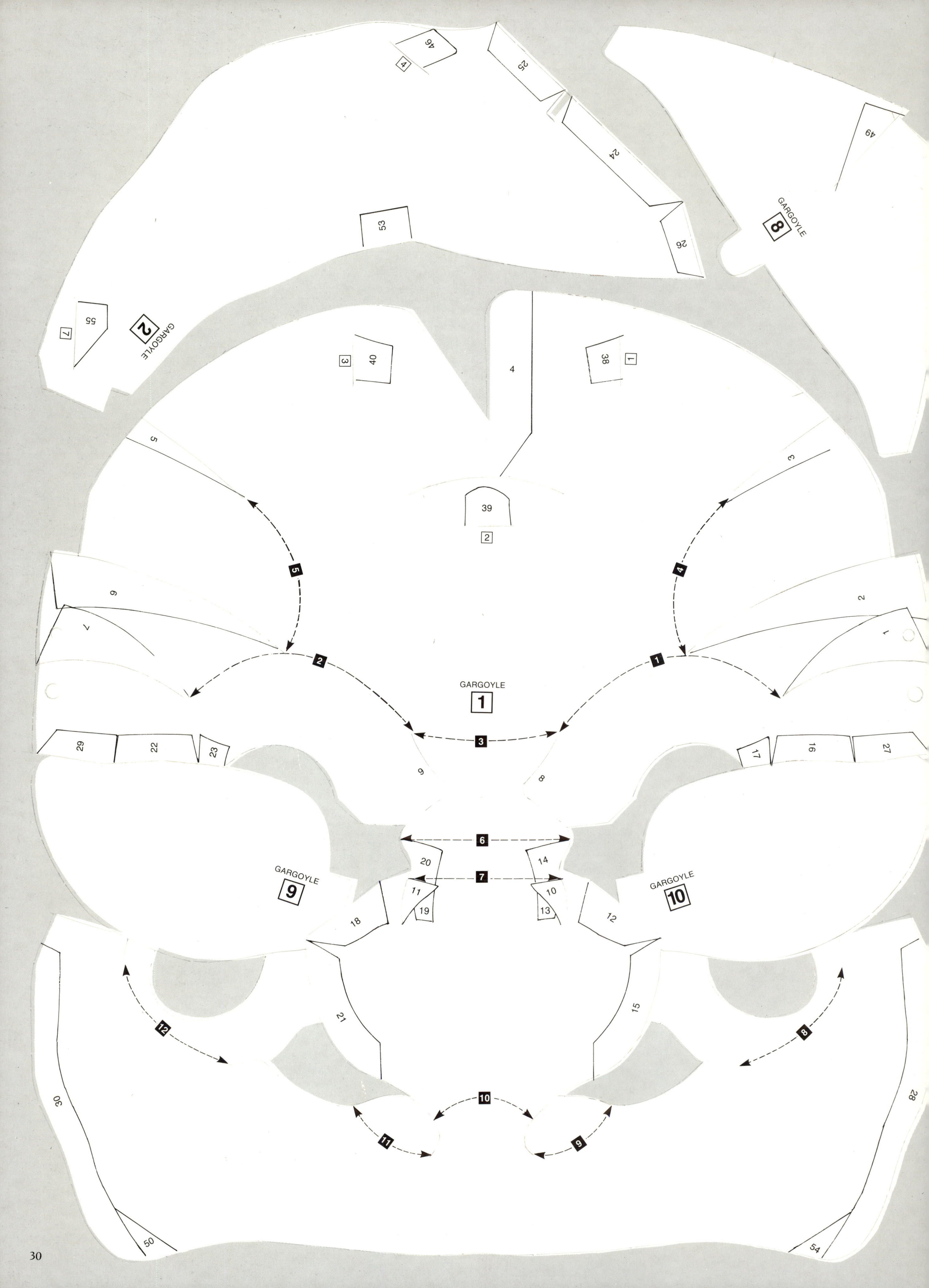
GARGOYLE 2
GARGOYLE 8
GARGOYLE 1
GARGOYLE 9
GARGOYLE 10

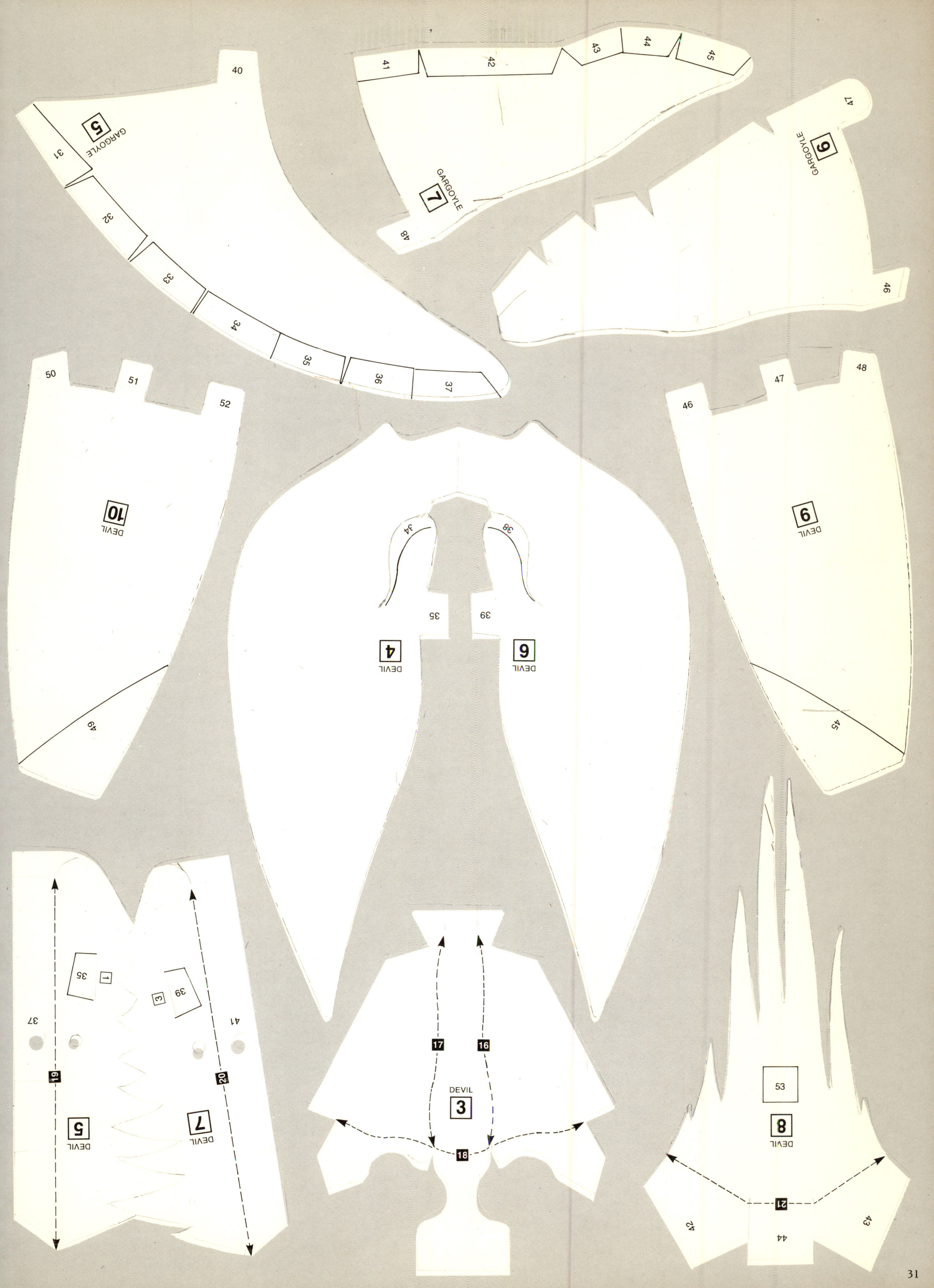
GARGOYLE 5
GARGOYLE 7
GARGOYLE 6
DEVIL 10
DEVIL 9
DEVIL 4
DEVIL 6
DEVIL 3
DEVIL 5
DEVIL 7
DEVIL 8

53
1
2
3
4
5
6
12
13
14
15
16
17
18
19
7
8
9
10
20
21
11

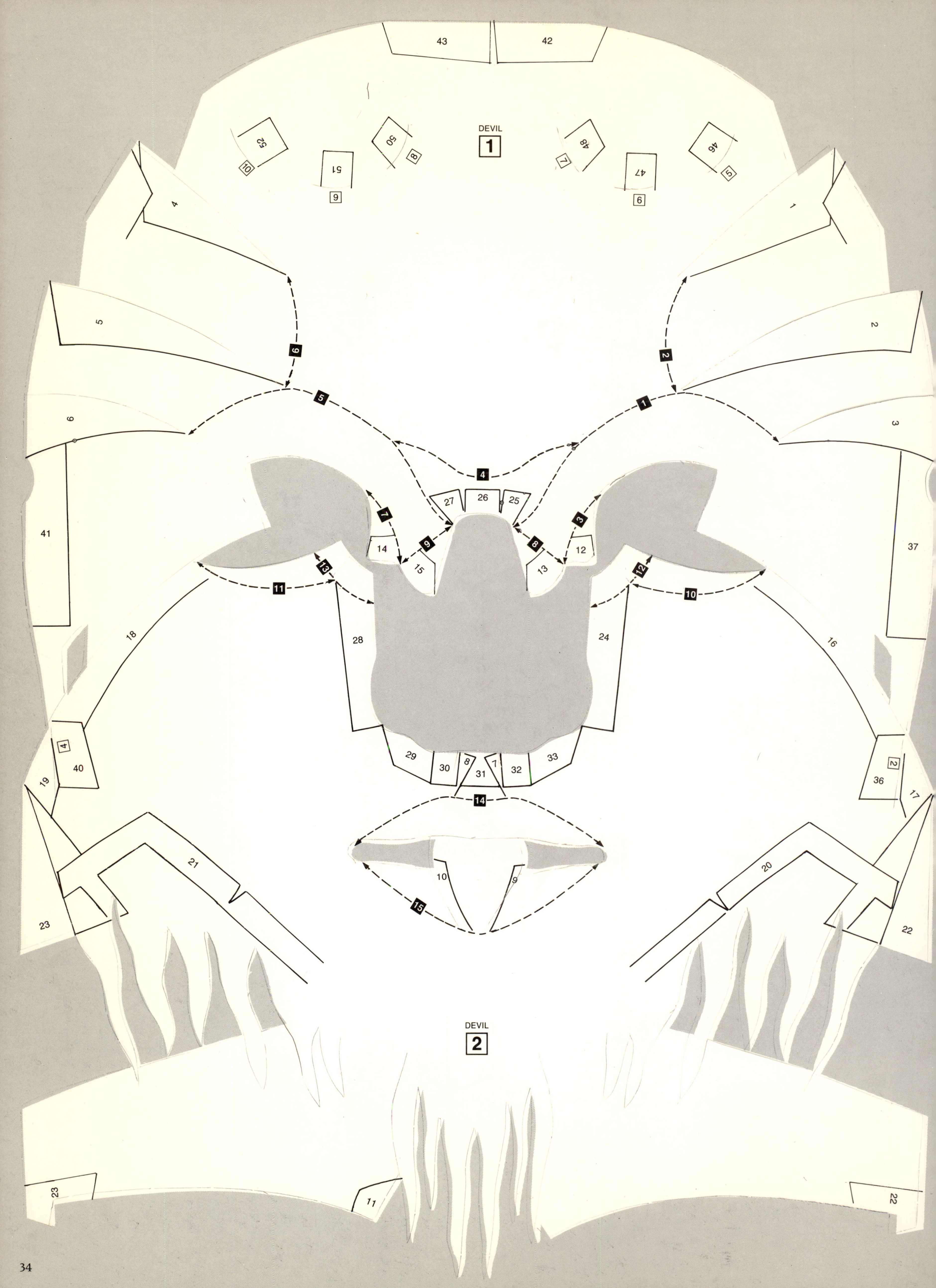
DEVIL
1
DEVIL
2

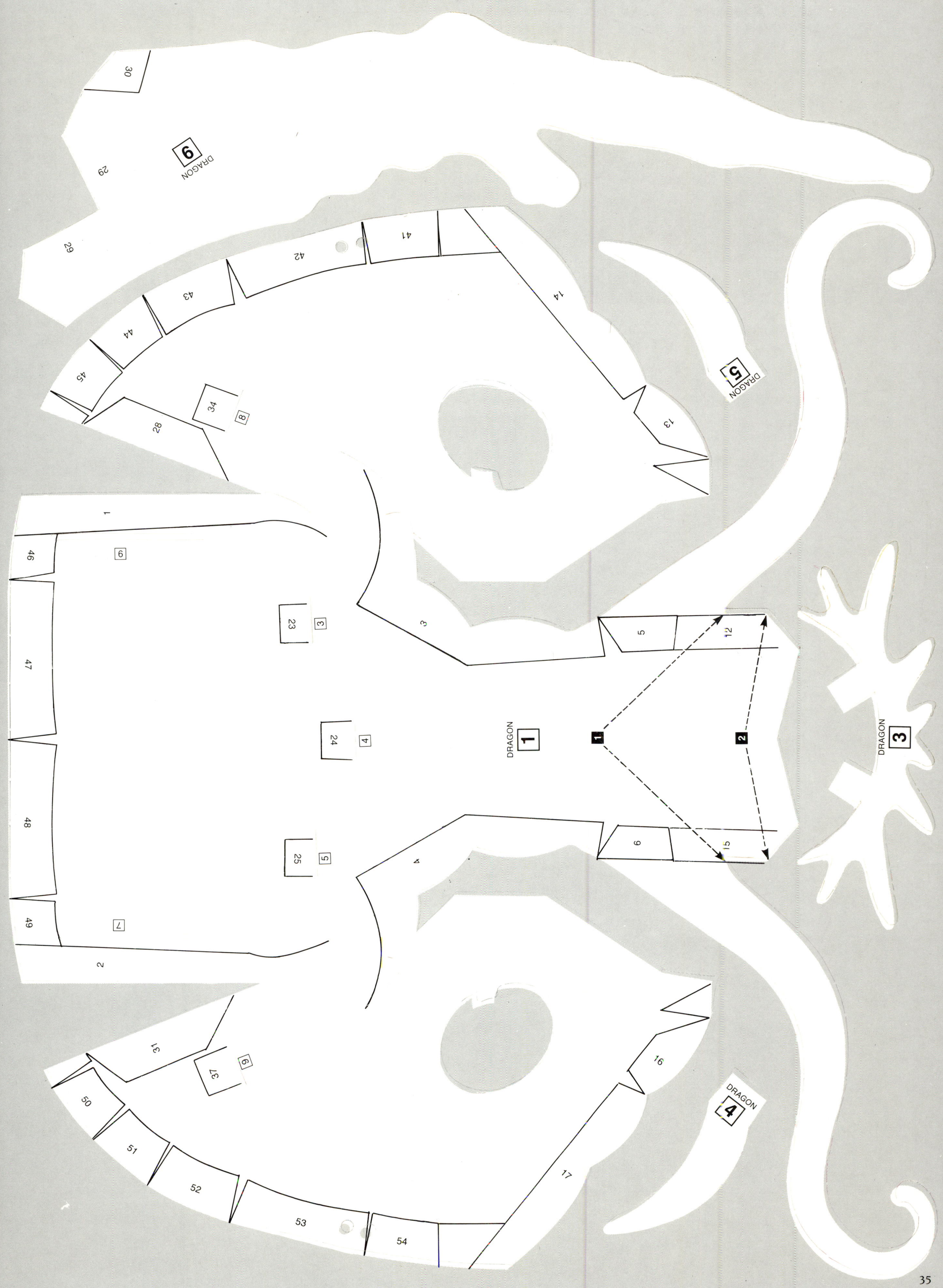
DRAGON 1
DRAGON 3
DRAGON 4
DRAGON 5
DRAGON 6

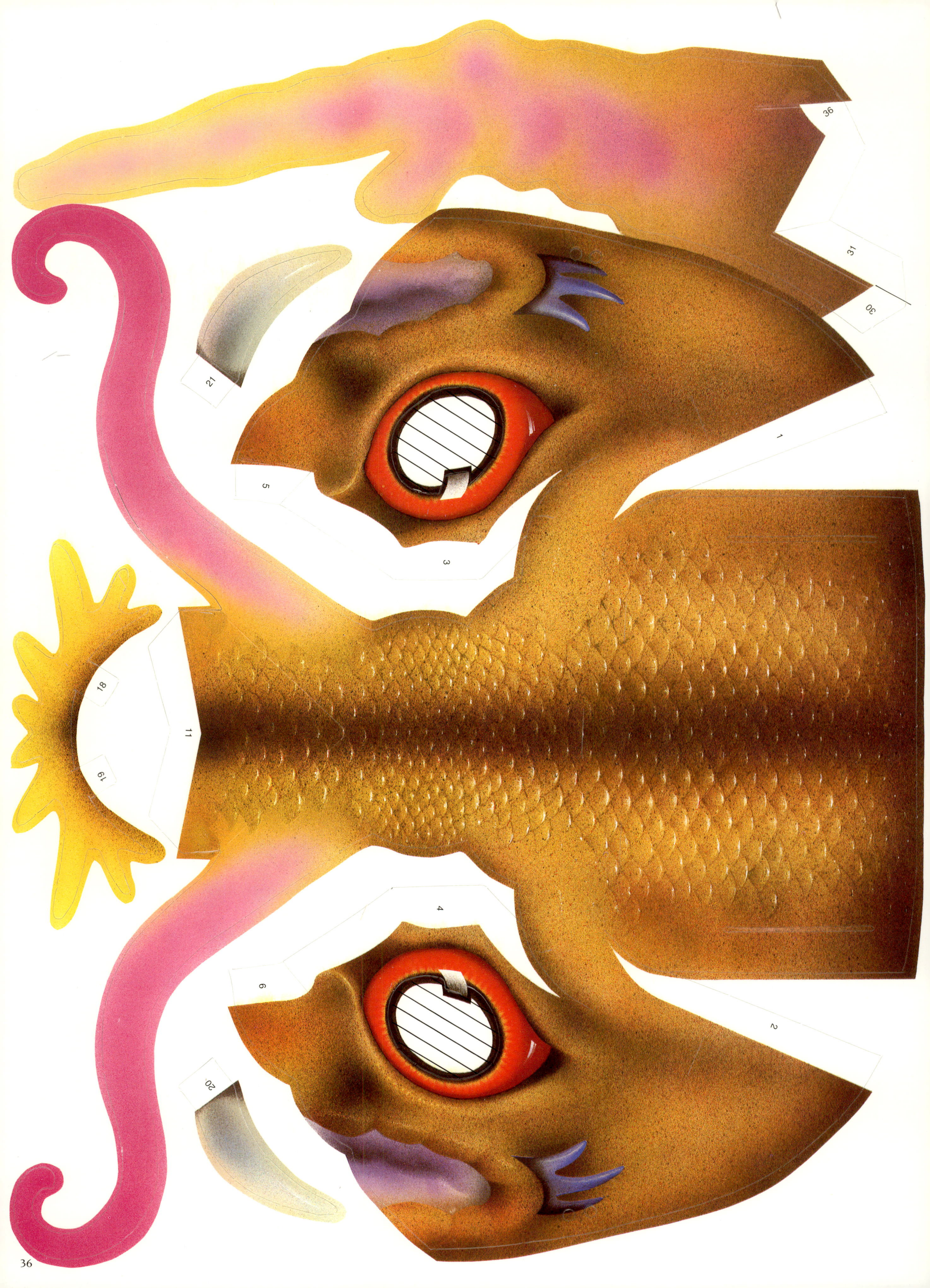

32
35
47
48
46
49
45
50
44
51
43
52
39
22
24
42
53
25
23
41
54
40
55
27
28
33

DRAGON 11
36
35
37
DRAGON 10
33
32
34
DRAGON 14
DRAGON 13
22
DRAGON 6
DRAGON 7
DRAGON 8
26
26
27

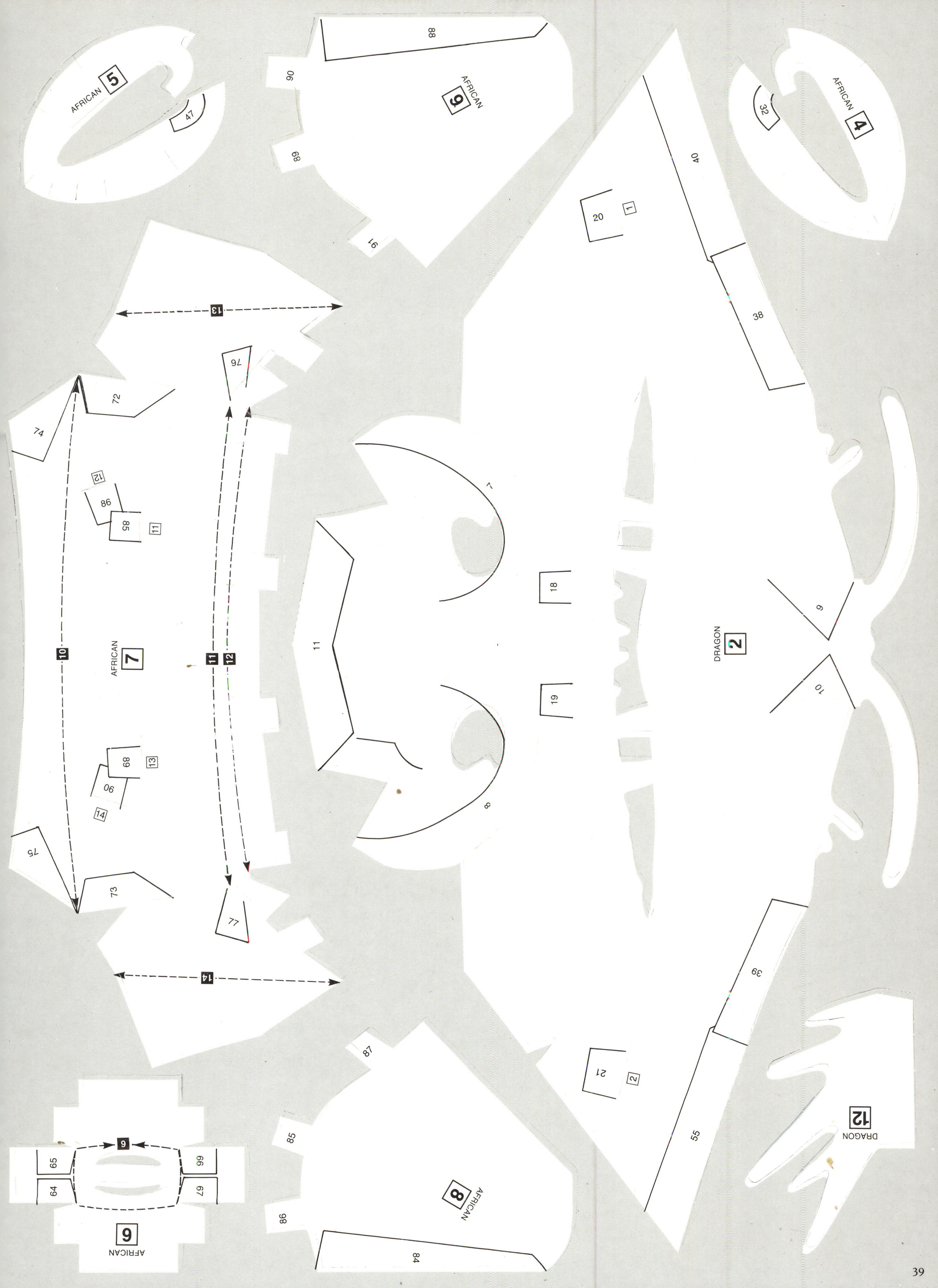
AFRICAN 5
AFRICAN 9
AFRICAN 4
AFRICAN 7
DRAGON 2
AFRICAN 8
AFRICAN 6
DRAGON 12

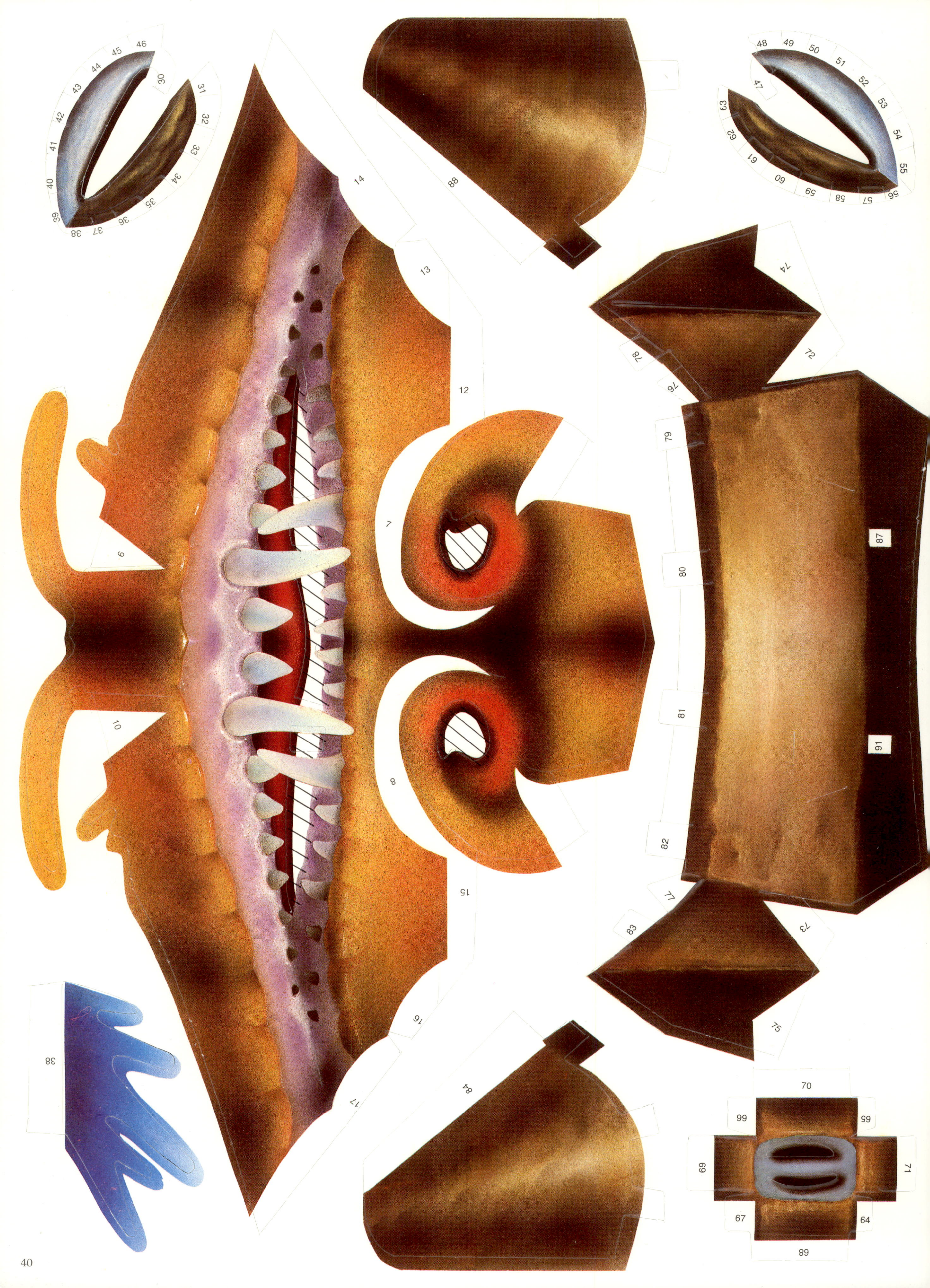

19
18
10
8
17
27
83
16
15
4
3
2
7
5
1
6
9
14
13
24
78
12
11

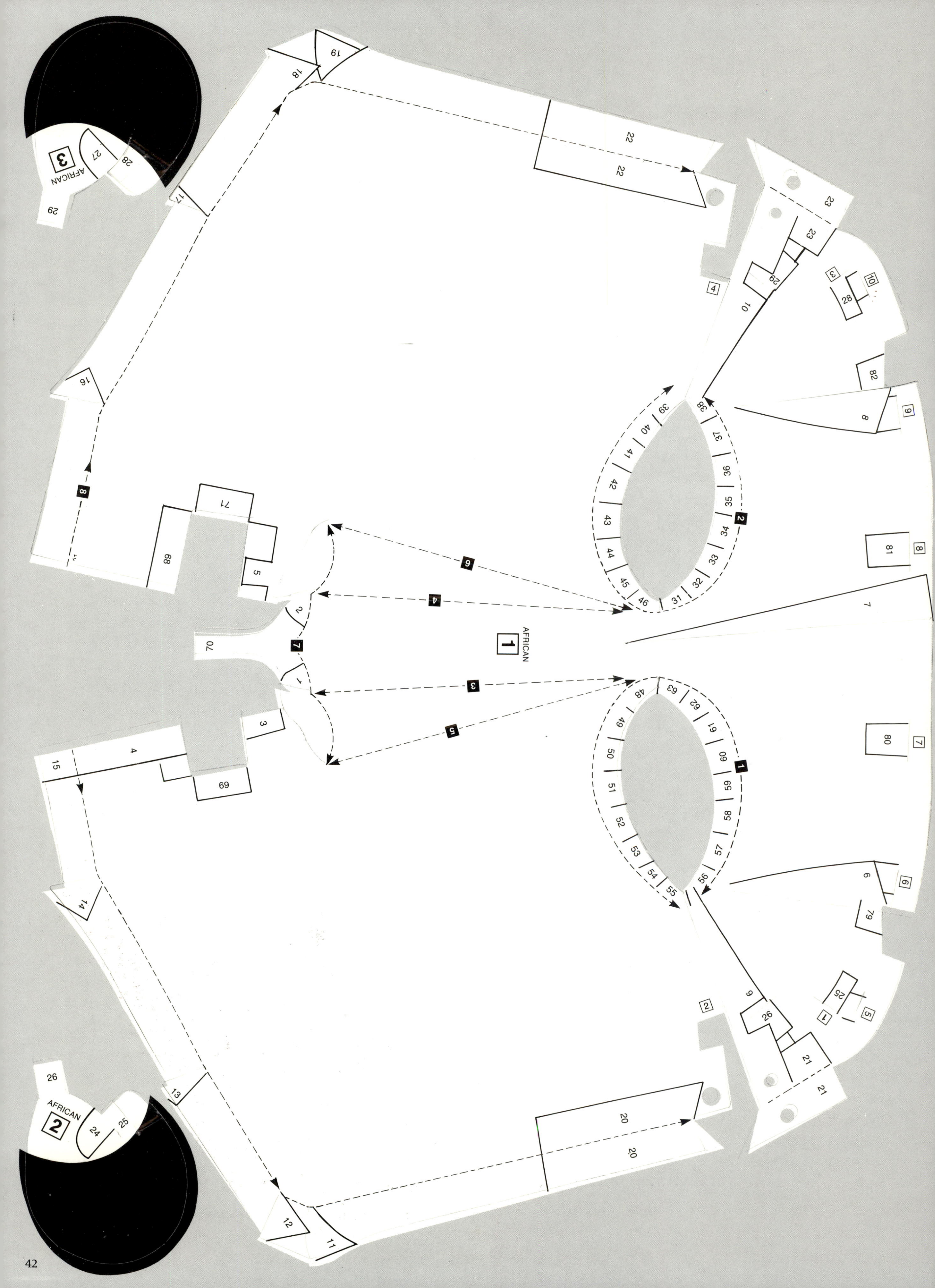

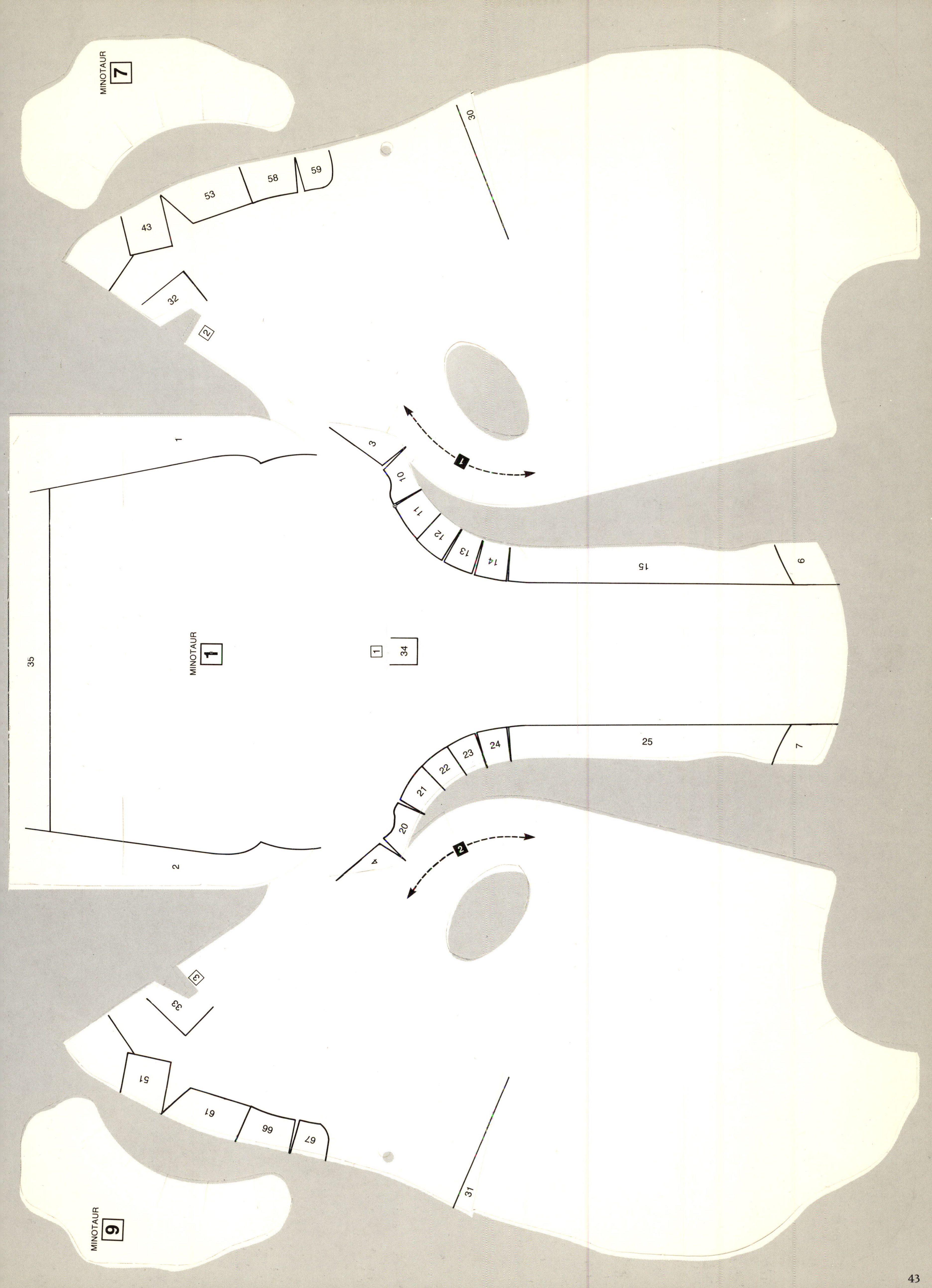
MINOTAUR 7
MINOTAUR 1
MINOTAUR 9

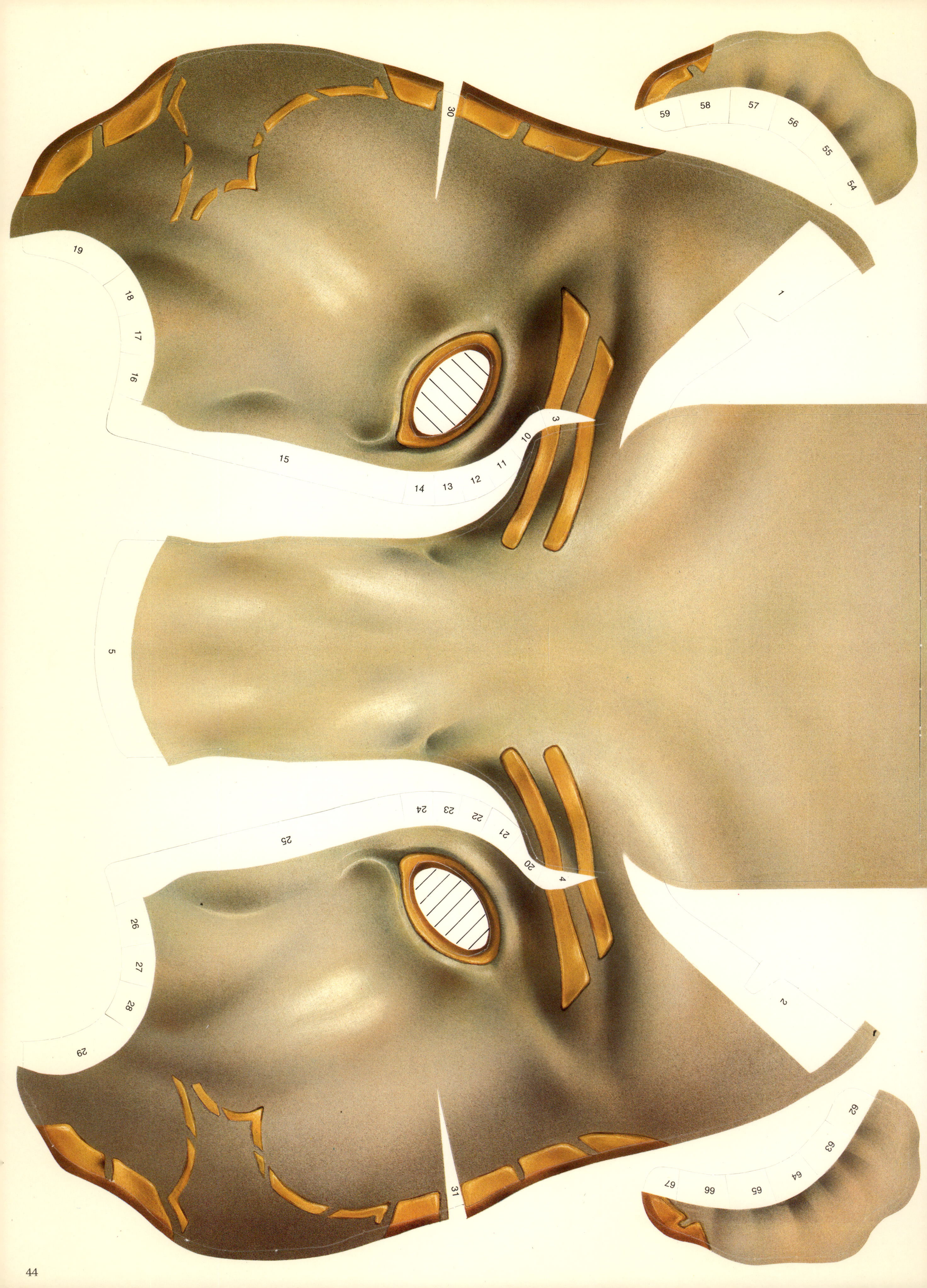
30
59
58
57
56
55
54
19
18
17
16
1
3
10
15
11
12
13
14
5
24
23
22
21
25
20
4
26
27
28
2
29
62
63
64
65
66
67
31

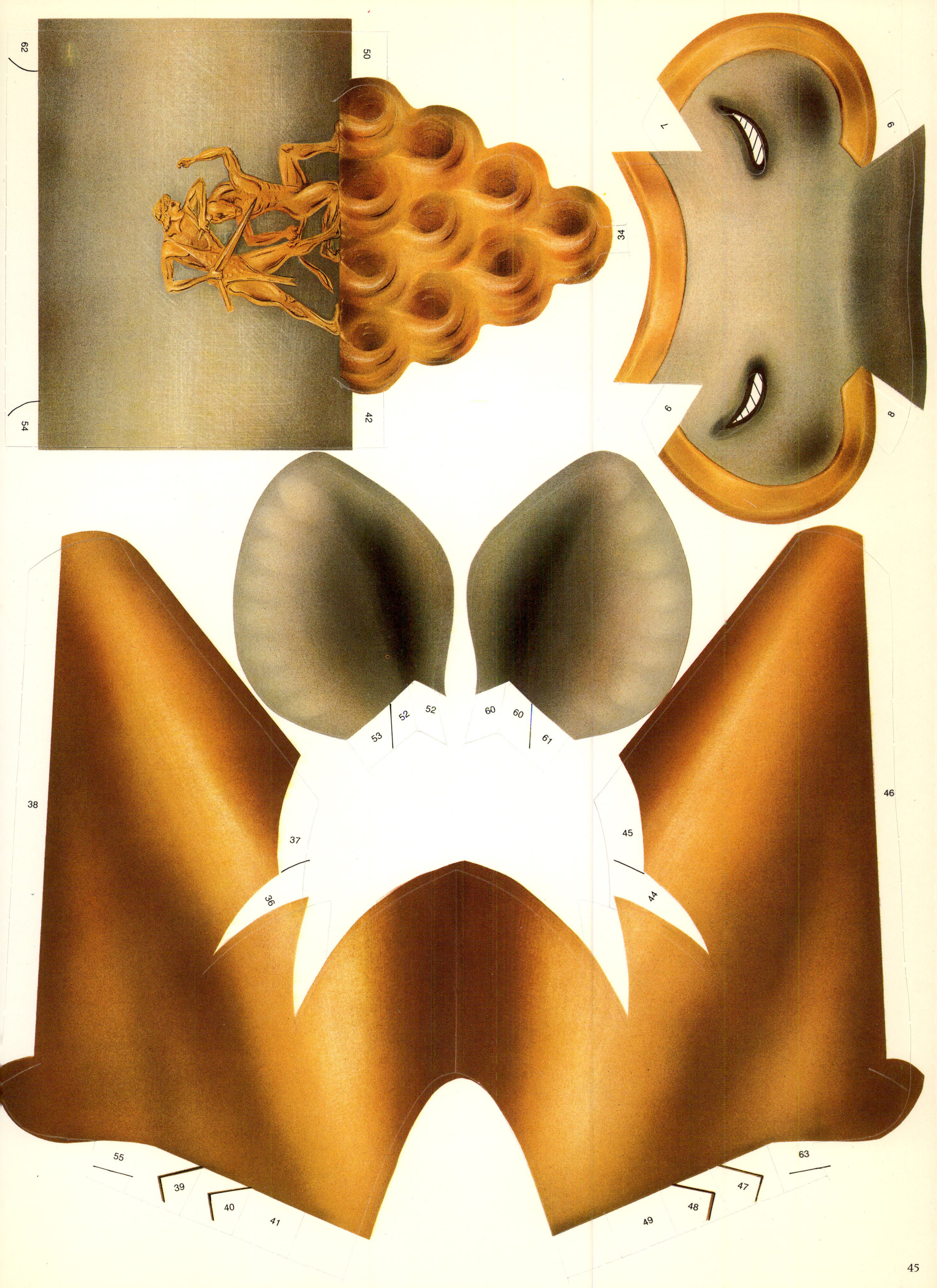
62
50
54
42
34
7
9
6
8
52
52
53
60
60
61
38
46
37
45
36
44
55
39
40
41
63
47
48
49

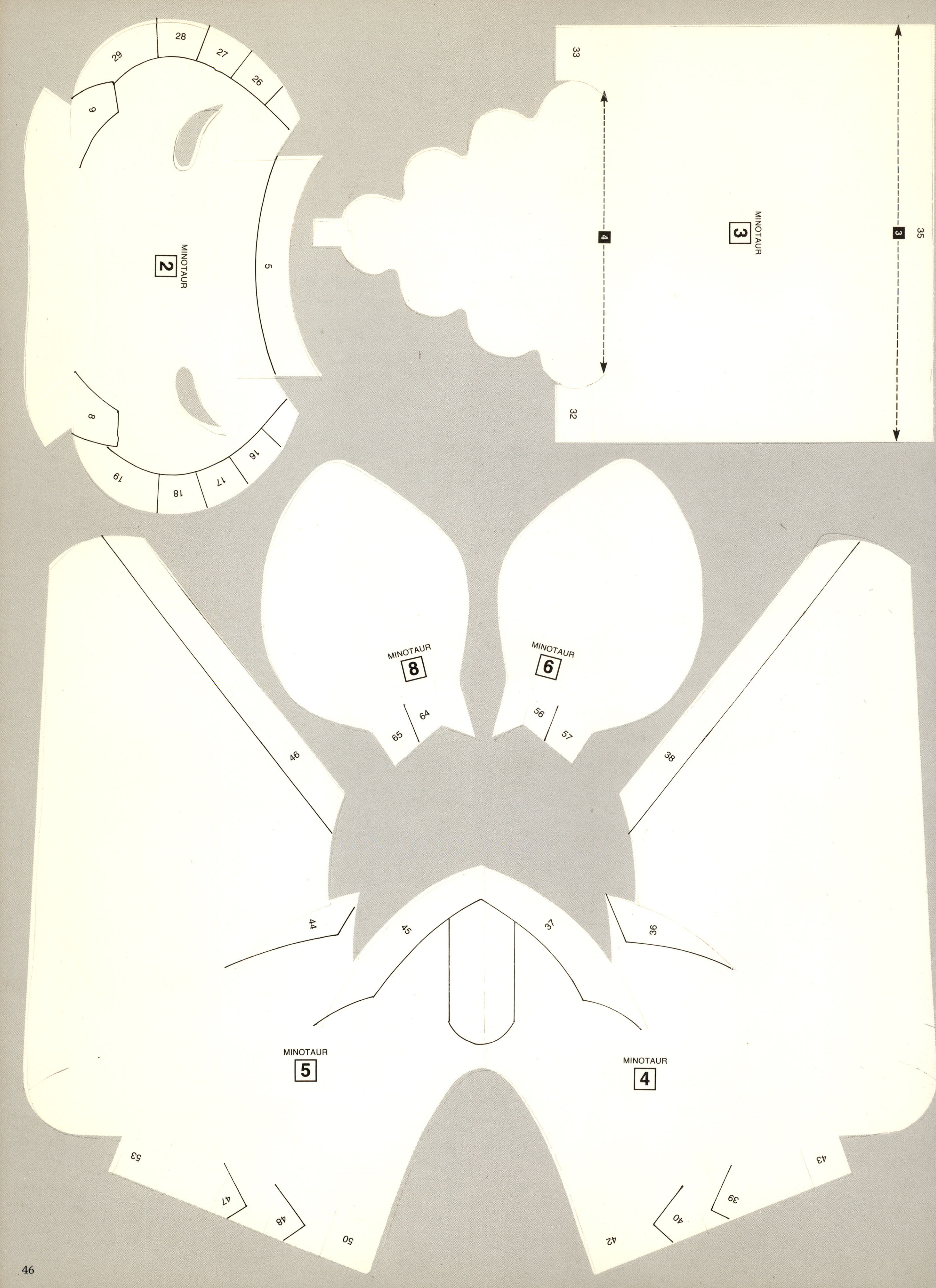
MINOTAUR
2
28
27
29
26
9
5
8
16
17
18
19
MINOTAUR
3
33
32
35
MINOTAUR
8
64
65
MINOTAUR
6
56
57
46
38
44
45
37
36
MINOTAUR
5
MINOTAUR
4
53
47
48
50
43
39
40
42

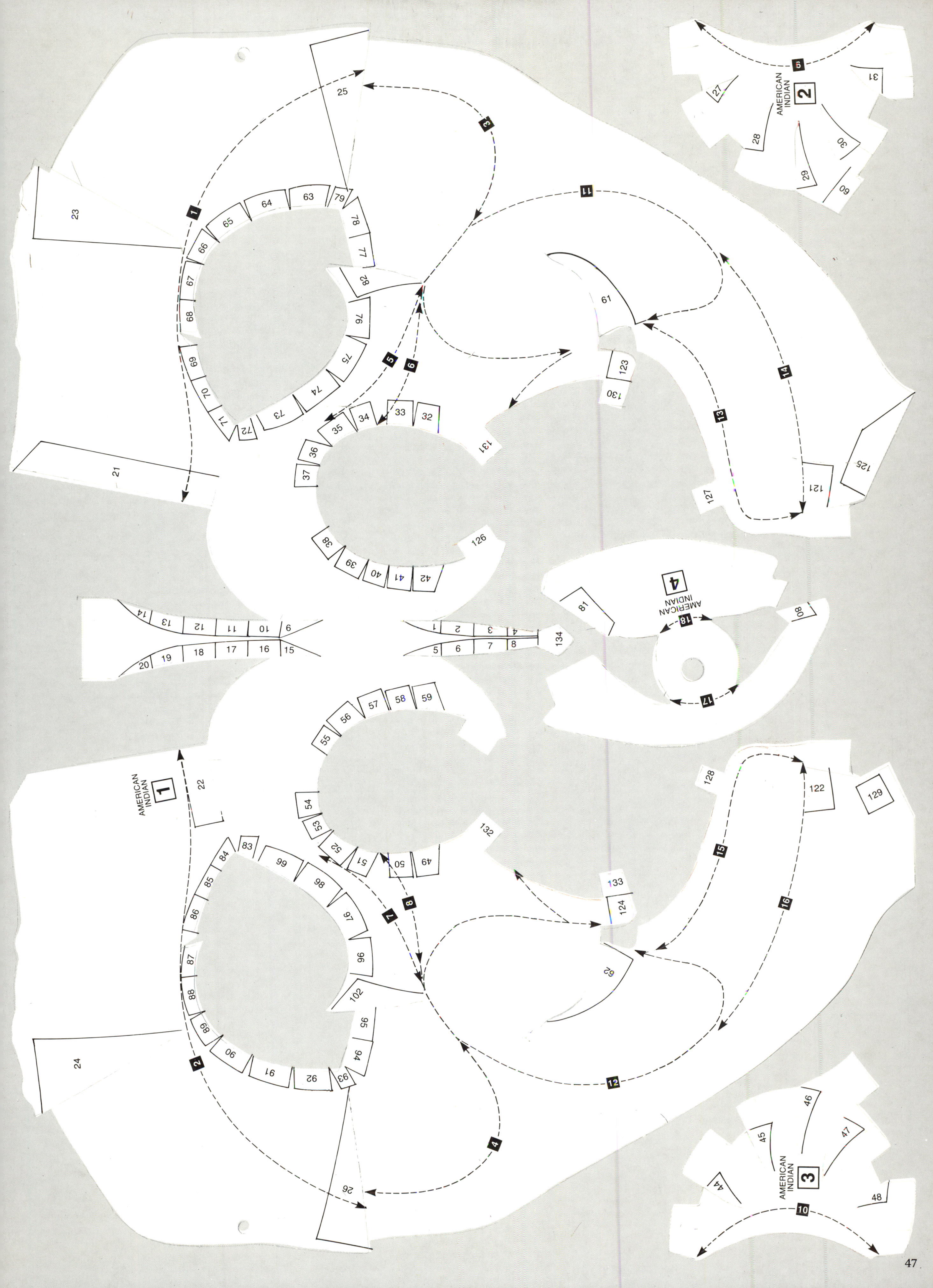

AMERICAN INDIAN 1
AMERICAN INDIAN 2
AMERICAN INDIAN 3
AMERICAN INDIAN 4

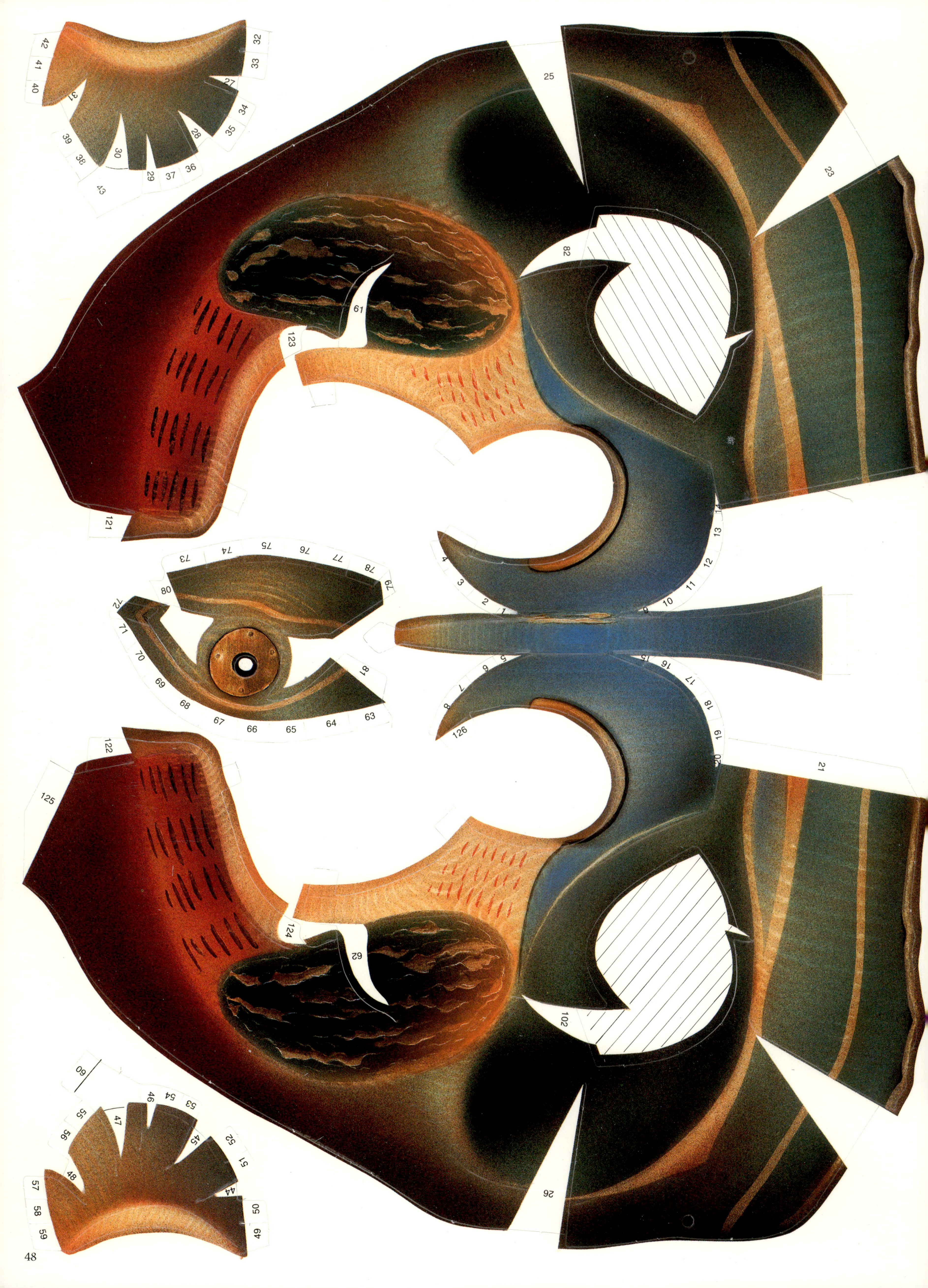

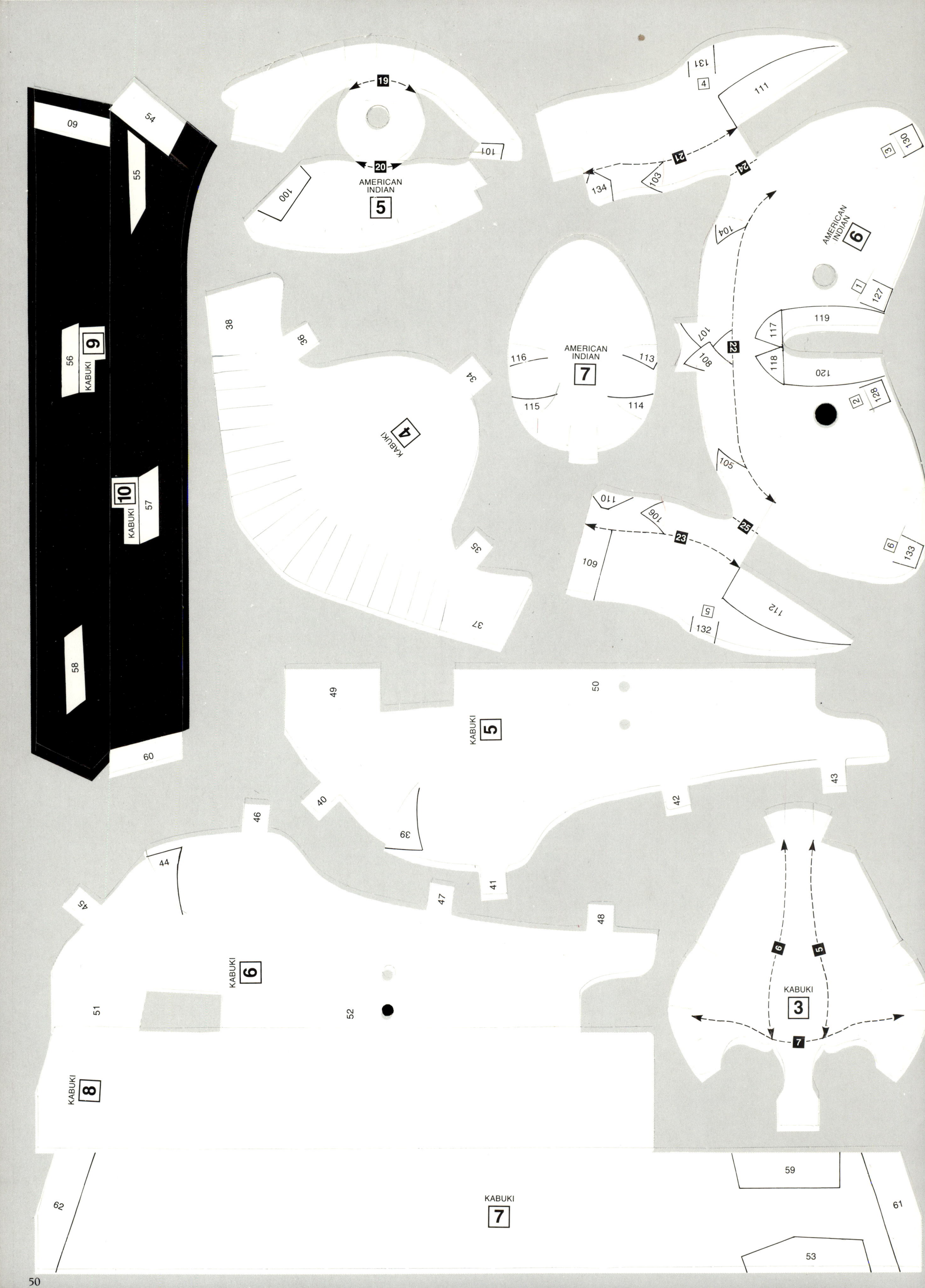
AMERICAN INDIAN
5
AMERICAN INDIAN
6
AMERICAN INDIAN
7
KABUKI
4
KABUKI
5
KABUKI
6
KABUKI
3
KABUKI
8
KABUKI
7
KABUKI
9
KABUKI
10